THE BUSH THEATRE PRESENTS
THE WORLD PREMIERE OF

Got To Be Happy

by Simon Burt
2 April – 3 May 2003

Directed by Owen Lewis
Designed by Lisa Lillywhite
Lighting design by Tanya Burns

thebushtheatre

Cast

Charley	Paul Copley
Caroline	Lisa Ellis
Richard	Martin Hancock
Connie	Polly Hemingway
Director	Owen Lewis
Set and Costume Designer	Lisa Lillywhite
Lighting Designer	Tanya Burns
Deputy Stage Manager	Sarah Hunter
Production Assistant	Rebecca Child
Assistant Stage Manager	Brett Parsons
Design Assistant	Penelope Challen
Set Construction	Bush Theatre Workshop
Press Representation	The Sarah Mitchell Partnership
	020 7434 1944
Marketing Consultation	Sam McAuley at Chamberlain McAuley
	020 8858 5545
Graphic Design	Emma Cooke at Chamberlain McAuley
	design@chamberlainmcauley.co.uk

This performance lasts approximately 1 hour 30 minutes plus interval.
Got To Be Happy received its world premiere at The Bush Theatre on 4th April 2003.

The Bush Theatre would like to offer special thanks to: Joanne Williams at Tchibo, Falcon Cooking Systems, Lloyd at LJ Scales and Tills.

2-4 CLAPHAM HIGH STREET LONDON SW4 7UT

Grill supplied by Falcon   Tables by Dentons

At The Bush Theatre

Artistic Director — Mike Bradwell
Executive Producer — Fiona Clark
General Manager — Brenda Newman
Literary Manager — Nicola Wilson
Marketing Consultant — Sam McAuley
Development Manager — Kate Mitchell
Production Manager — Pam Vision
Chief Electrician — Matt Kirby
Resident Stage Manager — John Everett
Assistant General Manager — Alex Mercer
Literary Assistant — Owen Lewis
Acting Literary Assistant — Frances Stirk

Box Office Supervisor — Dominique Gerrard
Box Office Assistants — Rowan Bangs
Sonia Beck
Johnny Flynn

Front of House Duty Managers — Kellie Batchelor
Caroline Beckman
Johnny Flynn
Muzz Khan
Rebecca Wolsey

Associate Artists — Biyi Bandele-Thomas
Es Devlin

*Pearson Writer in Residence — Simon Burt

Sheila Lemon Writer in Residence — Chloe Moss

*The Bush Theatre has the support of the Pearson Playwrights' Scheme sponsored by the Olivier Foundation

The Bush Theatre is the winner of the The Peggy Ramsay Foundation Project Award 2002

Paul Copley (Charley)

At The Bush: *Crossing the Equator, The Mortal Ash, Raping the Gold, Making Noise Quietly, German Skerries.*

Theatre includes: *Sing Yer Heart Out For The Lads, The Mysteries, The Ticket of Leave Man* (National), *The Contractor* (Oxford Stage Company), *Celaine, The Awakening* (Hampstead), *When We Are Married* (Chichester/West End), *With Every Beat* (West Yorkshire Playhouse), *The Servant* (Birmingham Rep, TMA Award 1995), *Prin* (Lyric Hammersmith/West End), *King Lear* (Anthony Quayle's Co), *Rita Sue, and Bob Too* (Royal Court), *For King and Country* (Mermaid, Olivier Award 1976).

TV includes: *The Key, Burn It, Hornblower* (3 series), *Dalziel & Pascoe - The Unwanted, Being April, Nice Guy Eddie, The Many Lives of Albert Walker, Peak Practice, Merseybeat, In Deep - Ghost Squad, Clocking Off, The Worst Witch, Holby City, Relative Strangers, Silent Witness - Gone Tomorrow, Queer As Folk, The Lakes* (2 series), *This Life* (2 series), *Casualty, Cracker* (3 series), *Roughnecks, A Pinch of Snuff, Harry, Rides, Heartbeat, Stay Lucky, Testimony of a Child, The Mistress, Oedipus at Colonus, Thunder Rock, Silas Marner, The Gathering Seed, Death of a Princess, Destiny, Treasure Island, The Secret Army, Chester Mystery Plays,* Diane and Ken Loach's *Days of Hope* (4 films).

Film includes: *Blow Dry, Driven, Jude, The Remains of the Day, War and Remembrance, Zulu Dawn, A Bridge Too Far, Alfie Darling.*

Lisa Ellis (Caroline)

Trained: Central School of Speech and Drama.

At The Bush: *The Danny Crowe Show* and *Normal.*

Theatre includes: *Be My Baby* (Soho Theatre Tour), *A Christmas Carol* (Chichester Festival Theatre), *Romeo & Juliet* (Creation Theatre Company), *The Miser* (Salisbury), *Moonshine* (Hampstead and Plymouth), *Trips* (Birmingham Rep) and *Popcorn* (West End).

TV includes: *Foyle's War, Midsomer Murders, Innocents, Holby City, Devices and Desires* and *The Story Teller.*

Film include: *Gangster No. 1* and *Simple Things,* and radio includes *Promises to Keep* (BBC) and *Little Angels* (BBC).

Martin Hancock (Richard)

Trained: Drama Centre

Theatre includes: *Edward II* (Glasgow Citizens), *Bleat* (Finborough), *Hoover Bag* (Young Vic)

TV includes: *The Bill*, *Wycliffe*, *This Life*, *London's Burning*, *Casualty*, *Our Mutual Friend*, *Coronation Street*, *First Sign of Madness*, *Keen Eddie* and *Doctors*. He has just finished filming *Bad Penny*, a children's series for the BBC.

Film includes: *The Milkman*, *The Only Game In Town*, *Liam*, *Daddy Fox* and *24 Hour Party People*.

Polly Hemingway (Connie)

Theatre: Polly won Best Actress Award for her performance in *Road* at the Royal Exchange Theatre, Manchester. She spent three years with the Northern Broadsides Theatre Company playing Queen Margaret in *Richard III* and Mistress Page in *The Merry Wives Of Windsor*. Other theatre includes *The Jew of Malta*, (Almeida), *All Credit To The Lads* (Crucible Sheffield), *I Licked A Slag's Deodorant* (Royal Court), *Lucky Sods* (West Yorkshire Playhouse), *A Chorus of Disapproval* (RNT), *Macbeth* (Riverside Studios), *Absolute Hell* (Orange Tree Theatre) and *Why Me?* (Strand Theatre).

TV Includes: *Trial and Retribution*, *Casualty*, *Wuthering Heights*, *The Bill*, *Where The Heart Is*, *Little Bird*, *Peak Practice*, *Midsomer Murders*, *Goodnight Sweetheart*, *The Locksmith*, *Ain't Misbehaving* and *Bare Necessities*. Polly was nominated Best Actress for *Dalziel & Pascoe* and for her performance of Gracie Fields in *Pride of Our Alley*.

Simon Burt (Writer)

Simon Burt was born in 1975 and studied drama at Loughborough University from 1994-97. He also attended writing classes with the Royal Court Young Writers Programme from 1999-2000. He was nominated by The Bush Theatre for a place on the 2001 Performing Arts Lab Writing For Younger Audiences Workshop and is currently the Pearson Playwright In Residence at The Bush Theatre. *Untouchable*, his first play, was produced by The Bush Theatre as part of the *Naked Talent* season in the autumn of 2002.

Owen Lewis (Director)

Owen's most recent production was the UK premiere of *Swimming in the Shallows* by San Francisco playwright Adam Bock. It enjoyed a successful run in London before the Edinburgh Festival 2002 (Pleasance Theatre). A regional tour is planned for autumn 2003.

His production of Moira Buffini's *Silence* at the Stephen Joseph Theatre, Scarborough, earned him the RSC Buzz Goodbody Award. He was Assistant Director to Jonathan Kent for *King Lear* at the Almeida, to Mike Bradwell for *Blackbird* at The Bush and spent eight months at Clwyd Theatr Cymru with Terry Hands and Tim Baker assisting on several shows, including Nicol Willamson's *King Lear*, *Accidental Death of an Anarchist* and *Flora's War*. He has also directed a number of rehearsed readings in venues across London including *Electricity* by Murray Gold at The Bush.

Owen is Literary Assistant at The Bush Theatre, an associate director of BrightChoice Productions (*Swimming in the Shallows*, *The Typographer's Dream*) and is a selector for the National Student Drama Festival.

Lisa Lillywhite (Designer)

Trained: Nottingham Trent University (Theatre Design)

At The Bush: *Blackbird, A Carpet, a Pony and a Monkey*

Theatre includes: *Live From Golgotha*, *PWA: The Diaries of Oscar Moore* (Drill Hall), *The Changeling* (Southwark Playhouse), *Modern Love* (QEH), *Passion* (Chelsea Theatre), *Young Hamlet* (Young Vic), *The Club* (Old Red Lion), *Musical Youth* (Birmingham Rep Studio), *Dutchman* (Ectetera Theatre), *The Local Stigmatic* and *The Dwarves* (Lyric Studio, Hammersmith), *He Stumbled* (collaboration with Howard Barker) National Tour.

Art Direction includes: Smash Hits Poll Winners Party, Evening Standard Film Awards, Mobo Music Awards, Pepsi Chart, Lloyds Fashion Week, Wicked Women Concert, Miss World .

Lisa has also assisted Es Devlin on *Henry IV part I & II* (RSC), *Meat* (Plymouth Theatre Royal), *Howie The Rookie* (The Bush) and *Hamlet* (Young Vic, Theatre Royal Plymouth ad Tokyo Globe).

Lisa was the winner of the Arts Foundation Scenography Award 2001 and was shortlisted for a Linbury Stage Design prize.

Tanya Burns (Lighting Designer)

Tanya was awarded the prestigious Arts Foundation Fellowship for Lighting Designers in 1996, and has since gained her MSc in Light and Lighting at UCL's Bartlett School of Architecture. In addition to theatre, she is now a lighting consultant on exhibition, architectural and environmental projects. Recent work includes; Samsung Centre, Moscow. Ford, Las Vegas, Nasdaq TV Studios, Times Square New York. Coca Cola at Madison Square Gardens, New York. Samsung Pavilion and Exhibition at the Winter Olympics, Salt Lake City, (International Gold Award Winner).

Tanya has worked for many years in British theatre, covering the West End, London and regional repertory theatres, lighting dance and opera as well as theatre. Her most recent work was for The Bush on the *Naked Talent* Season.

30 Years of The Bush Theatre

The Bush Theatre opened in April 1972 in the upstairs dining room of The Bush Hotel, Shepherds Bush Green. The room had previously served as Lionel Blair's dance studio. Since then, The Bush has become the country's leading new writing venue with over 350 productions, premiering the finest new writing talent.

Playwrights whose works have been performed here at The Bush include: Stephen Poliakoff, Robert Holman, Tina Brown, Snoo Wilson, John Byrne, Ron Hutchinson, Terry Johnson, Beth Henley, Kevin Elyot, Doug Lucie, Dusty Hughes, Sharman Macdonald, Billy Roche, Tony Kushner, Catherine Johnson, Philip Ridley, Richard Cameron, Jonathan Harvey, Richard Zajdlic, Naomi Wallace, David Eldridge, Conor McPherson, Joe Penhall, Helen Blakeman, Lucy Gannon, Mark O'Rowe and Charlotte Jones.

The theatre has also attracted major acting and directing talents including Bob Hoskins, Alan Rickman, Antony Sher, Stephen Rea, Frances Barber, Lindsay Duncan, Brian Cox, Kate Beckinsale, Patricia Hodge, Simon Callow, Alison Steadman, Jim Broadbent, Tim Roth, Jane Horrocks, Gwen Taylor, Mike Leigh, Mike Figgis, Mike Newell and Richard Wilson.

Victoria Wood and Julie Walters first worked together at The Bush, and Victoria wrote her first sketch on an old typewriter she found backstage.

In 30 years, The Bush has won over one hundred awards and recently received The Peggy Ramsay Foundation Project Award 2002. Bush plays have transferred to the West End and Broadway, and have been successfully adapted for film and television. Bush productions have toured throughout Britain, Europe and North America.

Every year we receive over fifteen hundred scripts through the post, and we read them all. According to The Sunday Times:

"What happens at The Bush today is at the very heart of tomorrow's theatre"

That's why we read all the scripts we receive and will continue to do so.

Mike Bradwell
Artistic Director
Fiona Clark
Executive Producer

COMING SOON

May 2003

Little Baby Nothing

By Catherine Johnson

Book online at www.bushtheatre.co.uk (no booking fee) or call 020 7610 4224

Support The Bush - Patrons Scheme
Be There At The Beginning

The Bush Theatre is a writer's theatre - commissioning, developing and producing exclusively new plays. Up to seven writers each year are commissioned and we offer a bespoke programme of workshops and one-to-one dramaturgy to develop their plays. Our international reputation of over 30 years is built on consistently producing the very best work to the very highest standard. We have a range of opportunities for individual and corporate giving which offer a close relationship with the theatre and a wide range of benefits, including ticket offers and invitations to special events. Help us to develop and produce the new writers and new plays of the future.

For more information please call Kate Mitchell, Development Manager on 020 7602 3703.

We would like to thank our current members and invite you to join them!

Rookies
Anonymous
Anonymous
David Day
Lucy Heller
Mr G Hopkinson
Malcolm & Liliane Ogden

Beautiful Things
Anonymous
Anonymous
Mr and Mrs Simon Bass
Clive Butler
Conway Van Gelder Ltd
Clyde Cooper
Patrick and Anne Foster
Mr Albert Fuss
Ken Griffin
Sheila Hancock
David Hare
Philip Jackson
Adam Kenwright
The Mackinstosh Foundation
Laurie Marsh
John Reynolds
Tracey Scoffield
Brian D Smith
Richard Zajdlic

Glee Club
Anonymous
Anonymous

Bronze Corporate Membership
Working Title Film/WT2

The Alternative Theatre Company Ltd
(The Bush Theatre)
Shepherds Bush Green, London W12 8QD
www.bushtheatre.co.uk
email: info@bushtheatre.co.uk
Box Office: 020 7610 4224

Registered company no 1221968
Registered charity no 270080.
Vat no 288316873

GOT TO BE HAPPY

Simon Burt

Characters

CHARLEY, *early sixties*

CAROLINE, *twenty-one*

RICHARD, *twenty-seven*

CONNIE, *late fifties*

The set is the kitchen of a pub with restaurant leanings. The white walls are yellowing in places, there isn't a lot of room, the place isn't a mess or disgusting but neither is the health inspector due anytime soon. There's an old wooden chair near a CD player which CHARLEY *likes to sit in on an evening. There are three doors. One next to the sink leads out onto a veranda piled with crates and bottles, the other two are next to each other on a right angle. One leads into the unseen pub, the other into the kitchen's unseen storeroom.*

CHARLEY: *chef, he looks like he's been working in kitchen nigh on forty year and more.*

CAROLINE: *waitress/barmaid, hangs about in doorways a lot.*

RICHARD: *chef/deputy, likes to lounge/sprawl about kitchen lording it. Likes to sit on work surfaces.*

CONNIE: *assistant helper, not used to manual kitchen work. She's a little incongruous in this setting.*

Scene One

Morning.

CHARLEY *enters from bar door ready for day's work. He carries a bunch of just going-off flowers which he puts straight into the bin along with some screwed-up paper used to wrap a fresh bunch.*

He takes off his coat, hangs it up, and goes to his little corner in the kitchen where he always puts his bag and stack of CDs. He opens the back kitchen door letting in summer sunshine air. He stands in doorway looking out. From the bar door CAROLINE *enters. She is in her dressing gown, bare feet.*

CAROLINE. Hiya.

CHARLEY. Hello love.

> CAROLINE *puts kettle on and gets out mugs for a brew.* CHARLEY *continues to look outside.*

CAROLINE. Been flower day has it?

CHARLEY. Aye. College day is it?

CAROLINE. No, not today.

CHARLEY. But it's Tuesday isn't it, that's college day isn't it?

CAROLINE. His lordship says it gonna be manic.

CHARLEY. Caroline!

CAROLINE. Oh don't start Charley.

CHARLEY. But it's summer, it always manic.

CAROLINE. Says he needs me.

CHARLEY. Never get yer exams, never get yer uni wi' out classes will you?

CAROLINE. God Charley anyone think you me Dad.

CHARLEY. Aye.

CAROLINE. They only revision classes, ones I already done like.

CHARLEY. Aye but these classes helping ya wi' passing exam?

CAROLINE. Charley, you aren't saying ought that isn't whizzing round my noggin you know?

CHARLEY. Sorry love, won't say no more.

CAROLINE. . . . Charley?

CHARLEY. Yeah?

CAROLINE. His lordship's got another assistant starting. Soz.

CHARLEY. 'Nother bloody chancer working in here?

CAROLINE. Just over the summer, but he's gonna yank yer chain about it.

CHARLEY. Would expect nought less. How young?

CAROLINE. Dunno.

CHARLEY. They do at least know what a knife an' fork is?

CAROLINE. I dunno. You know what he like. Hire a foetus if he thought it could do job . . . I just warning ya. If you wanna yank his chain about it.

CHARLEY. I will.

CAROLINE. But don't go too far. It be you he bollocks when it gets manic, an' I'm tired so chances of me making a huge cock-up are way up there, so dead cert I –

CHARLEY. Caroline Caroline, ssshh. 'Ey?

CAROLINE. Aye.

CAROLINE takes look in bin – horrified.

Charley! For fuck's sake!

CHARLEY. Caroline the swearing –

CAROLINE. No. What you putting these fresh un's in bin for?

CAROLINE *pulls the flowers back out of the bin and rearranges them into shape.*

What you been putting on grave bloody seeds? You can't put them in bin, where you get idea they're going off?

CHARLEY. Are by my standards.

CAROLINE. Your standards are weird. Well least you could have left them on yer mate's grave 'nother day fine. These aren't going to waste. I'm putting them out in bar.

CHARLEY. In the bar?

CAROLINE. One each on restaurant tables. Aye, they'll go nice there.

CHARLEY. They been on a grave!

CAROLINE. They don't know.

CAROLINE *wanders back out into bar taking flowers with her.* CHARLEY *watches her go and shakes head bemused. He strolls out onto veranda and takes in the glorious day . . .*

RICHARD *enters from bar door, also in dressing gown and barefoot carrying the retrieved flowers and stuffing them straight back into the bin.* CAROLINE *follows him in and tries to go about making a brew.*

RICHARD. Oi Charley?

CHARLEY. What?

RICHARD. Them flowers, they're ones off of your flower day aren't they?

CAROLINE. No.

RICHARD. They bloody are. You always putting these uns on graves aren't you?

CHARLEY. I'm saying nought.

RICHARD. Why didn't you stop her?

CAROLINE. What's wrong with 'em?

RICHARD. You know what is. We not having them on tables after where they've been. Bloody dead corpses keeping them rosey an' daisy.

CAROLINE. All flowers are kept rosey by the dead.

RICHARD. Not wi' the dead only few feet right under them they ain't! You getting these teas brewed?

RICHARD *wanders out onto veranda less impressed by glorious day than* CHARLEY. *He lights a fag and puffs away directly into* CHARLEY*'s face.*

Wish you'd stop giving her ideas.

CHARLEY. Nought do with me.

RICHARD. Yer flowers. You bloody throw 'em away before you get 'ere right? Between churchyard and here.

CHARLEY. Yes Richard.

RICHARD. Sure you got enough CDs wi' you today?

CHARLEY. I am. Good acoustics this time year.

RICHARD. It's not Abbey Road.

CHARLEY. Caroline got classes?

RICHARD. Nought important.

CHARLEY. That good. It gonna be right hot, we could need her.

RICHARD. Charley – god's sake! Been running this kitchen five year gimme some credit, course I got her in.

CHARLEY. She not missing ought important is she?

RICHARD. I said. Only revision ones.

CHARLEY. Sound important.

RICHARD. None of your fucking business right?

CHARLEY. Right.

RICHARD. Right . . . say Caroline!

CAROLINE. What?

RICHARD. Yer classes, not missing ought important like are you? All hands to pump on chuffing hot day like this isn't it?

CAROLINE. No nought important.

RICHARD. See? Revision, repeats. She be alright. She did right good in them mocky practice thingys. She right good like that is my Caroline.

CHARLEY. Yes Richard.

CAROLINE *brings out two cups of tea, one for each of them.*

Ta love.

CAROLINE *now goes and gets her cup of tea – re-joins them . . .*

Going to be hot today.

RICHARD. Gonna be hot.

CAROLINE. God you right chuffing merchants of doom you two, you never know it might piss it down later.

RICHARD. Nah.

CHARLEY. Way up in seventies I heard.

RICHARD. Touching eighties I heard.

CAROLINE. Chuffing buggery.

CHARLEY. Beer garden gonna be chocka. Be worse than '76.

CAROLINE. Good six year 'fore my time Charley.

RICHARD. I were a toddler then.

CHARLEY. Shifts from hell they were.

RICHARD. Oh aye, shifts from Krakatoa's arse they were!

CHARLEY. They were I tell you!

RICHARD. Fucking chuffa nora . . . ey, but we'll lose few pounds from round midrift won't we Charley?

CHARLEY. I don't need lose ought. Lose mine all in sweat slaving at coal face here.

RICHARD. Oh you're a right martyr you are aren't you?

CHARLEY. Got me battle scars to prove it.

CHARLEY is showing them something on his elbow.

Off a cooker December 1980 that is. Went bad septic an' all.

RICHARD waves a hand in CHARLEY'S face.

RICHARD. Hello! Remember this you bastard maimer! When ya put sodding hot plate on me hand? That not gone neither. That never go.

CHARLEY. How many time I sorry, but that's not a scar.

RICHARD. It fucking is!

CHARLEY. That's not a scar, this is a scar!

CHARLEY turns and pulls shirt up a little, trousers down a little revealing something that makes RICHARD and CAROLINE make loud revolted noises and take a few feet away.

CAROLINE. Fed up of seeing that. Every time you bend over fat fryer I see that.

CHARLEY. You get one one day Richard you will. Law of averages. 19 –

RICHARD. – 87, I know you bastard I know.

CHARLEY. Looks like yesterday don't it? I know about pain me.

CAROLINE. I know, I heard yer music.

CHARLEY. You what?

CAROLINE. No! – sorry Charley, sorry sorry didn't mean it!

CHARLEY. What getting up your Caroline? She don't usually have a go at me music?

RICHARD. She think yer music shite don't she, like me.

CAROLINE. No I don't it just slipped out, I don't think that at all.

RICHARD. She think same as me. Shit.

CAROLINE. I don't.

RICHARD. Shut up you daft mare.

CHARLEY. Shouldn't you be dressed by now? We open in fifteen minutes. Ray be about, he'll have you, bollock pair of you.

RICHARD. Nah. We got it covered.

CHARLEY. No! You got tables to lay girl and you should be sorting veg out shouldn't ya?

RICHARD. 'Ey! I'm boss, I get to shit down line right? Anyway it's covered.

CAROLINE. It is.

CHARLEY. What is?

RICHARD. I've told Ray.

CHARLEY. Told Ray what?

RICHARD. I really laid it out to him –

CAROLINE. Stop messing with him. Tell him.

CHARLEY. Tell me what?

CAROLINE. He did lay it out to Ray, I were there.

CHARLEY. What out?

RICHARD. Getting extra help in.

CHARLEY. Off a' Ray?

RICHARD. Even Ray's realised summer lunches too manic just for three of us. Laid it out to him, need help I said. Bad like.

CHARLEY. And?

RICHARD. Ray says he got pennies for an assistant.

CHARLEY. Oh aye? An' who might this bloody chancer be? When they starting?

RICHARD. In about five minutes.

CHARLEY. Five . . . five, we gonna be right manic and you bringing in chuffing dead wood for us to carry? Chuffing – how young this time? Can they reach top shelf in fridge?

RICHARD. Aye! An' she isn't young, she old.

CAROLINE. Old?

RICHARD. Aye. Old.

CHARLEY. One extreme to other wi' you, we no room for a zimmer in here!

RICHARD. You're not exactly in first fucking flush yerself! She only your old, not right old.

CHARLEY. This is my kitchen this is!

RICHARD. It isn't!

CHARLEY. Forty year I been in here, in way that matter it mine and you bringing in chuffing dead wood, we have a routine in here.

RICHARD. Since when?

CHARLEY. Since always.

RICHARD. Well always is over. Roll on my transfer. I tell you Caroline when I've got me own gaffe, if this were me own gaffe I'd fire him. Tell you what Charley, when I get me own gaffe out Bradford way you come work for me, an' I'll fire you. I'll like that. Then I'll hire you again, an' fire you again. Hire you fire you with emphasis on the firing like. I'd like that.

CHARLEY. I'd have you for unfair dismissal.

RICHARD. Fucking try me.

CHARLEY. I would.

RICHARD. You'd be on.

CHARLEY. Me an' all.

CAROLINE. Charley?

CHARLEY. Yeah?

CAROLINE. That enough now.

CHARLEY. Couldn't I yank him bit more?

RICHARD. You what?

CAROLINE. He getting testy.

CHARLEY. I getting into me stride here love.

CAROLINE. Go on, bit more then.

RICHARD. Thick as bloody thieves you two.

CAROLINE. Aye.

CHARLEY. Aye.

RICHARD. So she can work here?

CHARLEY. Aye.

CAROLINE. Aye.

RICHARD. Us lot been stuck in here too long.

CHARLEY. Aye.

CAROLINE. Aye.

RICHARD. Stop it!

CHARLEY. Well come on, if she starting in five minutes hadn't you better tell me who hell she is? What kind of drag factor am I working with here?

RICHARD. I said! Just old housewife, her husband snuffed it about a year back.

CHARLEY. So she'll get all blubby then when it gets manic. Great.

RICHARD. She be alright.

CHARLEY. Bet she blubs.

RICHARD. She won't. She's bored, must be to end up here. She won't be bothered 'bout bein' manic. She wants the manicness.

CAROLINE. God, hope I never get that lonely.

CHARLEY. And what's she called?

RICHARD. Connie, something.

CHARLEY. Connie?

RICHARD. Aye.

CHARLEY. Her husband dead a year back?

RICHARD. Yeah I said.

CHARLEY. Bit posh? Posher than us like?

RICHARD. Aye. That her . . . what?

CHARLEY. She isn't working here.

RICHARD. Ey come on, knock it off now.

CHARLEY. No I serious, she isn't.

RICHARD. You what?

CAROLINE. Charley?

CHARLEY. What she be wanting job for?

RICHARD. I don't know, I dunno, said she wanted it.

CAROLINE. She only one that applied.

RICHARD. Good enough for me.

CHARLEY. I serious here.

RICHARD. No you not. Quit wi' yer yanking now.

CHARLEY. No I am. She isn't.

RICHARD. Caroline – will you get said to him to cut it out! He don't know when –

CAROLINE. Charley?

CHARLEY. She isn't.

RICHARD. Charley . . . she is!

CHARLEY. She isn't.

CAROLINE. Charley. Come on now.

Doorbell goes.

RICHARD. That be her . . . now stop it wi' yer yanking . . . you yanking me right?

CHARLEY. . . . Aye. Make no difference if I weren't would it?

RICHARD. No it wouldn't.

RICHARD *goes out into bar to answer it.*

CAROLINE. Charley, what you like? Pissing him off 'fore manic shift?

CAROLINE *looks through the little glass window in the kitchen door.*

Ey up. She pretty, for oldish, aye, bit posh an' all by looks . . . She don't wanna wear them clothes in here.

CHARLEY *goes to the window nudging* CAROLINE *out of the way and having a look. Comes away.*

CAROLINE. That her? . . . Who you think it is?

CHARLEY. I were yanking you.

CAROLINE. No you weren't . . . you can't . . . well what you think she be like in here? Ought good? Bad? Big drag factor? How you think she deal wi' Richard's monk ons? . . . Charley? . . . God I know what Richard means – can't tell ought wi' you no more.

CAROLINE *tosses coffee down sink, puts out fag.*

RICHARD *enters from bar followed by* CONNIE *wearing coat and carrying handbag.*

RICHARD. You can hang yer stuff up there cos it's hanger-like. This is my Caroline.

CAROLINE. Hiya.

CONNIE. Hello.

CAROLINE. That's Charley.

RICHARD. Aye, an' that's Charley.

CAROLINE. Charley?

CHARLEY. Hiya . . . hello.

CONNIE. Hello.

> CHARLEY *goes deep back into work.*

RICHARD. Aye. Well we'll start wi' scrubbing this table down, right manky it is, needs good scrub 'fore riot starts.

CONNIE. Riot?

RICHARD. Customer bastards. Charley show you cloths.

CONNIE. Yes.

RICHARD. Right, I need shower.

CHARLEY. Aye.

> RICHARD *leaves out into bar. After a moment* CAROLINE *follows.*
>
> CONNIE *tentatively approaches* CHARLEY *who has his back to her.*

CONNIE. Cloths.

CHARLEY. Huh?

CONNIE. Cloths? Please.

CHARLEY. They're under the sink.

> CHARLEY *gets her a cloth from under sink and passes it to her making sure their hands do not touch. She starts gently wiping the table down, takes some crumbs to put in bin. Opens bin, sees flowers.*

CONNIE. You done your flowers this morning . . . I be doing mine in a few days.

CHARLEY. Right.

CONNIE. You never let yours go off. I like the carnations you put on. I put a posey on myself.

CHARLEY. I know you do . . . what you doing here?

CONNIE. I'm wiping the table down.

CHARLEY. Right. Be opening soon. Best get on with it.

They go about their work, CONNIE *continues to give table a scrub but it is clear she isn't overly used to this kind of work. Rather gentle scrubbing.*

You be needing some hot water an' soap to give that a good scrubbing.

CONNIE. Yes . . . is there a bucket?

CHARLEY *gets small bucket and fills it with water and soap. While water fills they try not to look at each other but fail.* CHARLEY *passes her the bucket making sure their hands do not touch. They go about their work.*

Scene Two

The lunchtime shift is heating up. CONNIE *is preparing salads and side orders.* CHARLEY *is shoving things in the cookers.* RICHARD *is dishing up meals for* CAROLINE *to take out.*

RICHARD. Okay. Go go go!

CAROLINE *takes two of the meals,* RICHARD *follows with the other two out into the bar. After a few moments* RICHARD *returns. The ticker machine goes, he takes it.*

It two hickories. How you doing Connie?

CONNIE. Fine fine.

RICHARD. You doing great with them salads there. See Charley, only hire class me!

RICHARD *gets two baguettes from under the top grill and starts cutting them, slapping cheese and chicken into them.*

We enough baguettes?

CHARLEY. Aye.

RICHARD. No we haven't!

CHARLEY. What you asking me for then? Just say get more baguettes in.

RICHARD. You seen orders for Hickories, get 'em under chuffing grill.

CHARLEY gets a big bag of baguettes and puts them in the microwave to defrost.

Alright alright! Don't go mad on 'em. An' don't be getting cob on wi' me either!

The ticker goes, CHARLEY *gets it.*

Bugger! What is it?

CHARLEY. Big grill.

RICHARD. Bastard! You do that?

CHARLEY. Aye.

RICHARD takes baguettes out of microwave slaps them under the top grill. CAROLINE *enters with an untouched steak meal.*

CAROLINE. She don't want it medium.

RICHARD. Fuck!

CHARLEY. How's she want it?

RICHARD. Do not say rare, do not say rare.

CAROLINE. Rare.

RICHARD. Bastard bitch! Fuck her!

He makes rude gestures in direction of bar.

CHARLEY. Keep it warm, we still get shut of it.

CHARLEY *puts steak under the top grill.*

RICHARD. Not bloody likely.

RICHARD *takes steak from top grill and wangs it in bin.*

Caroline, take salads out.

CAROLINE *is rifling through previous order slips.*

RICHARD. Caroline the salads. Connie, you do us some more chicken an' sauce for the hickories, chicken in there.

CONNIE. Okay.

RICHARD. In fridge . . . there love there!

CONNIE *opens fridge, looking up and down shelf.*

Middle shelf middle shelf!

CONNIE *finds Tupperware containing chicken.*

That yer chicken, now yer sauce, top shelf top shelf!

CONNIE *starts looking amongst Tupperware on top shelf.*

Caroline what fuck you doing?

CAROLINE. It isn't Charley's fault. It mine. I got it down wrong, got numbers wrong.

CHARLEY. Don't worry about it.

RICHARD. Caroline I don't give a shit, the salads.

CAROLINE. It were me.

CHARLEY *leaves what he is doing, goes to* CONNIE *at fridge and finds her the right Tupperware box with sauce in it, opens it and hands it to her.*

CONNIE. Thank you.

CHARLEY *goes back to his work.* CONNIE *puts the sauce and chicken into the baguettes rather delicately.*

RICHARD. Alright it were you. The salads. Ey? Come on!

CAROLINE. It weren't Charley.

CAROLINE *takes the salads out.*

RICHARD. You still cooked it medium didn't you?

CHARLEY. Aye.

RICHARD. Your fault.

During following CAROLINE *enters getting more orders and leaves.* CHARLEY *goes to the CD player.*

RICHARD. Ey! You can leave that alone. Watch yer chips!

CHARLEY. It soothing.

RICHARD. Well it winds me up. It shite.

> CAROLINE *re-enters looking for more orders, lingers a moment listening.* RICHARD *watches* CAROLINE *go, then he switches radio to some rock poppy music and cranks the volume up a notch.*

Now this is soothing.

The ticker goes.

Arrrgghh! . . . Connie, come on love, you gonna have to pick the pace up there. Come on.

> RICHARD *steps in taking* CONNIE's *work away from her, slapping chicken and sauce into a baguette.*

It isn't a bairn's arse you know, get it slapped in.

> RICHARD *does one and then leaves it back to* CONNIE *who makes a pitiful attempt at slapping stuff into a baguette.* RICHARD *seems to step away from it all, both physically and mentally. He goes out onto the veranda. Leans on crates, head down.*

CHARLEY. Richard! . . . Richard! . . . Come on . . .

> RICHARD *comes back in.*

RICHARD. One of these days, I'm gonna go out on that veranda, when it manicest it ever been an' I'm gonna walk down them steps an' never come back . . . or I'll go down pool hall.

CHARLEY. You won't even do that.

RICHARD. No. I won't.

> CAROLINE *enters only to be handed a Hickory baguette by* CHARLEY *who bustles her back out.*

CAROLINE. Where this for?

CHARLEY. Table eight.

RICHARD. What wi' you getting her back out there?

CHARLEY. Nought.

RICHARD. She sticks up for you you daft – I can bollock her if you like? I'll call her back in and bollock her. She keep sticking up for you I might just.

CHARLEY. You never bollock your Caroline.

RICHARD. No I bollock you.

Ticker goes which RICHARD *grabs.*

Two steak pies.

He goes into the storeroom.

CONNIE. Are you alright?

CHARLEY. Aye, fine.

CONNIE. Thank you for –

CHARLEY. Don't do that.

CONNIE. What?

CHARLEY. Talking as if we're familiar.

CONNIE. I'm only asking.

CHARLEY. We're not familiar.

CONNIE. We are.

CHARLEY. No we not.

CONNIE. But our flowers.

CHARLEY. Me an' you, we not familiar.

Goes back about his work.

Scene Three

Early evening.

CHARLEY *and* CONNIE *are finishing tidying up for the day, wiping quickly round sink or something. A simple classical CD plays quietly in corner.*

CAROLINE *enters dead on her feet, lighting a fag.*

CAROLINE. It never pissed it down.

CHARLEY. No.

CAROLINE. You're good Connie. Where you been all me working life? Isn't she Charley?

CHARLEY. Aye. Very good.

CAROLINE. That high praise from him that . . . you coming back tomorrow?

CONNIE. I will.

CAROLINE. Bloody hell Charley. Richard hasn't scared her off. Miracle in itself that isn't it?

CHARLEY. Aye.

CAROLINE. Made of stern stuff you Connie . . . so . . .

CONNIE. Yes?

CAROLINE. You known Charley a while haven't you?

CHARLEY. Caroline.

CAROLINE. Alright that weren't subtle but you won't say and me curiosity, it like getting blood out of a stone wi' you isn't it?

CONNIE. It is.

CAROLINE. Aye it is isn't it?

CONNIE. Yes.

CAROLINE. So? How long you known him?

CONNIE. Well I knew him when he was your age.

CAROLINE. An' you were?

CONNIE. Gosh, I be, seventeen, eighteen.

CAROLINE. What? God. That be near forty year like? I can't even imagine that. An' our Charley, young, can't imagine that neither.

CONNIE. Oh he was.

CAROLINE. What were he like?

CONNIE. He rode a motorbike.

CAROLINE. A motorbike? Him?

CONNIE. Aye.

CAROLINE. But they move. Fast like.

CONNIE. Well he did move. It was a big Harley Davidson he'd saved and saved for.

CAROLINE. How long you save for it Charley?

CHARLEY. I don't know.

CAROLINE. A long time?

CHARLEY. Aye.

CONNIE. And leathers, black shiny leathers.

CAROLINE. Oh god, and now I'm seeing Charley now like, in leathers like, too weird.

CONNIE. He used to thrash his leathers about in the yard here out the back and ride his bike over them.

CAROLINE. So he were tapped in head then? What for?

CONNIE. So they'd look lived in. Battered.

CAROLINE. He were posing! You were posing?

CONNIE. He were a poser.

CAROLINE. Poser! . . . You a poser Charley?

CHARLEY. I weren't that much.

CONNIE. Don't you believe him, he were a poser.

CAROLINE. Charley! So where did you used to ride this bike then?

CONNIE. Out Holmfirth way most, ey Charley?

CAROLINE. Charley?

CHARLEY. Aye, good terrain up there.

CAROLINE. An' you went with him?

CONNIE. Sometimes.

CAROLINE. So you were romantic like? . . . Riding up there, must have had your arms wrapped round him ey?

CONNIE. We did all that Charley and me. He were scared of that bike you know. He only rode it to impress me.

CAROLINE. Did you? God, were you scared?

CHARLEY. You got to be scared, or you'd be stupid an' fall off it.

CONNIE. What happened to the bike?

CHARLEY. I fell off it.

CONNIE. Did you?

CHARLEY. Aye.

CAROLINE. Were you alright?

CHARLEY. Me leathers protected me.

CONNIE. And the bike?

CHARLEY. If you fall off you got to get straight back on. I didn't.

CONNIE. Oh. You always rode too fast.

CHARLEY. Aye – Caroline, alright? Can you stop wi' the twenty questions now?

CAROLINE. Just asking.

CHARLEY. Aye well, me an' her, aye, randy buggers right? That what you wanna know?

CAROLINE. Yeah . . . okay.

CHARLEY. Well go on then, haven't you tables or something that's nought to be getting on with eh?

CAROLINE. Are you shitting down the line on me Charley? Me?

CHARLEY. I am shitting down line. I got seniority over you an' I'm using it so go on.

CAROLINE. Alright, bloody use it then. See what I have to put up with Connie, monky –

Bar door opens, RICHARD *pokes head through.*

RICHARD. Caroline! Rush on in bar.

CAROLINE. There only four in the queue.

RICHARD. But we due mystery customer bastard aren't we?

CAROLINE. How can it be mystery if brewery tell you he's fucking coming? That cruel that is.

RICHARD. Will you get behind bar? Please?

CAROLINE. See Connie? Monky, an' right monky.

CAROLINE *leaves.* CHARLEY *continues about his work,* CONNIE *looking for a way into his attention.*

CONNIE. You shouldn't speak to her like that.

CHARLEY. I speak to her hows I like.

CONNIE. No you don't. You speak nice to her, I know you do.

CHARLEY. Aye.

CONNIE. Just because I'm here there no need to take it out on her.

CHARLEY. I don't.

CONNIE. She was only asking.

CHARLEY. Aye an' you were saying stuff. I don't like it.

CONNIE. She's lovely.

CHARLEY. Aye.

CONNIE. How long she been here?

CHARLEY. Five, nearly six year. With him.

CONNIE. I hear she's leaving.

CHARLEY. Aye.

CONNIE. Him as well?

CHARLEY. Aye.

CONNIE. Off to university isn't she?

CHARLEY. Aye.

CONNIE. To do what?

CHARLEY. History.

CONNIE. Oh, what's she going to do with it?

CHARLEY. Don't know.

CONNIE. He's going with her?

CHARLEY. Aye.

CONNIE. . . . They living in another pub?

CHARLEY. Aye.

CONNIE. Are . . . are you going to talk to me?

CHARLEY. I am.

CONNIE. No. You're answering me.

CHARLEY. . . . She says teaching when he's about. He likes to have idea where they're heading, and . . . look I know what you just been doing.

CONNIE. What have I been doing?

CHARLEY. Using our Caroline to get all familiar with me. Well you can stop it. I've said we're not familiar.

CONNIE. If we working together we going to get familiar.

CHARLEY. But I don't want you working here. I don't understand . . . there were a time in post office fifteen year back when you blanked me an' we were next to each other in the same fucking queue for fifteen minutes. Not a flicker from you. There never been ought from you when I see you in street. Nought from day we split. An' here you are, oh hello! What?

CONNIE. There been nought from you.

CHARLEY. Aye but, I thought we knew where we stood . . . look, I'm sorry about your David, I truly am, not that I knew him like but he were far too young to be dying and leaving you, I'm right sorry for you –

CONNIE. I don't want you to be sorry for me.

CHARLEY. What do you want?

CONNIE. A little job over the summer, something to do. Something that's mine.

CHARLEY. But love, you not cut out for this job.

CONNIE. I know.

CHARLEY. You done plenty of cooking haven't you?

CONNIE. Course I have. Been housewife haven't I? It just different in here.

CHARLEY. Aye.

CONNIE. I'll get better.

CHARLEY. He might be a tit but he's right, wi' the baguettes, you got to wang it in you know.

CONNIE. I'll try harder with the, wanging.

CHARLEY. They none the wiser out there, you gotta be no messing about.

CONNIE. I know.

CHARLEY. You will get better.

CONNIE. I want you to talk to me.

CHARLEY. What about?

CONNIE. Anything.

CHARLEY. You only here cos you lonely.

CONNIE. No I want this job, but I do want you to talk to me . . . I see you tomorrow?

CHARLEY. Aye.

> CONNIE *gets her things and leaves.* CHARLEY *wanders out onto the veranda and sits on crate.* RICHARD *and* CAROLINE *enter,* RICHARD *goes out on veranda and looms over* CHARLEY *who carries on smoking defiantly.* CAROLINE *hangs in storeroom doorway.*

I want me quiet time.

RICHARD. You gonna be long?

CHARLEY. No, but I not had me quiet time yet.

RICHARD. But me an' my Caroline wanna, you know.

> RICHARD *heads back into the kitchen, he sees* CAROLINE *by storeroom doorway and lifts his hands up in despair but tries to lead* CAROLINE *into the storeroom.* CHARLEY *can hear them.*

RICHARD. He won't hear ought.

CAROLINE. No.

RICHARD. He won't.

CAROLINE. No! . . . Connie gone?

RICHARD. Aye. No point standing there then, he not going anywhere while yet bastard.

CAROLINE. Richard leave him.

RICHARD. He is.

CHARLEY (*shouting through*). I'm not going anywhere wi' out having me quiet time. Work bloody hard I do. Tie knot in it or I tell Ray I know what goes on in that storeroom. Don't you think I bloody won't!

RICHARD (*also shouting through kitchen to veranda*). An' you can tell Ray you known what going on in storeroom last five year an' all! Please him chuff loads won't it?

CHARLEY. I will!

RICHARD. An' I'll tell him his pub's such a creaking shit hole we can't shag in our own bed!

CAROLINE. Richard!

CHARLEY. I will tell Ray! 'Nother bollocking don't bother me.

RICHARD. Ey ey ey Charley come on, now come on don't say ought here you can't take back. Ray finds out –

CHARLEY. Oh aye, going all soft an' diplomatic like now aren't you? No! You gimme me quiet time, half hour, piss off pair of ya!

RICHARD *looks as if he is about to reply but a pleading look from* CAROLINE *makes him think otherwise.*

CAROLINE. Look, it don't matter, I'm knackered, an' I revision to do.

RICHARD. I'll be off down pool hall then, you fancy coming?

CAROLINE. No. Revision.

RICHARD. Just game of pool like, like we used to?

CAROLINE. No . . . Richard?

RICHARD. Yeah?

CAROLINE. Don't be bollocking him in front of Connie.

RICHARD. Why?

CAROLINE. He likes her.

RICHARD. Does he?

CAROLINE. Yeah.

RICHARD. Nah.

CAROLINE. I know likes when I see it.

RICHARD. I'm a boss. Who else am I meant to bollock?

CAROLINE. Bollock me, I don't care.

RICHARD. What you mean you don't care? Course you would. I want you to care.

CAROLINE. You wouldn't want bastard regional manager bollock you front of me?

RICHARD. I'd deck him first.

> CAROLINE *shrugs "told-you-so" at him.* RICHARD *kisses her on lips,* CAROLINE *doesn't really reciprocate.*

Pool hall's open late tonight.

CAROLINE. Yeah.

RICHARD. Enjoy yer shift.

> RICHARD *leaves out bar door.* CAROLINE *stays in doorway . . . switches light off.* CHARLEY *sees light is off and thinks he is now alone. He wanders into the kitchen, pulls out his usual chair, puts CD in player and Dido's lament starts. He turns up the volume so it fills the room.* CAROLINE *doesn't know where to put herself until –*

CAROLINE. You alright?

> CHARLEY *bolts around startled, then sees it is* CAROLINE *and calms a little, but he turns the music down quieter than before.*

CHARLEY. Aye.

CAROLINE. Don't worry. He's gone down pool hall. I'm only on me break, you get yer quiet time.

> CAROLINE *wanders round to him.*

That sounded nice, pretty . . . for your music.

CHARLEY. It is.

CAROLINE. I'm sorry what I said 'bout yer music.

CHARLEY. What were that?

CAROLINE. 'Bout it bein' crap.

CHARLEY. You didn't say crap.

CAROLINE. No, I said shit. Soz.

CHARLEY. You didn't say shit, he said shit.

CAROLINE. Well, that were him talking, not me.

CHARLEY. I know.

CAROLINE. You an' her were talking lovely when I left you. You like her don't you? I mean you still like her, don't you?

CHARLEY. Aye.

CAROLINE. . . . Aye. So who'm I gonna tell if you tell me like eh? An' me an' Richard gone soon anyway so – got you there haven't I? Tell me? Well you used to take her for motorbike rides. Says likes to me that does.

CHARLEY. She's lonely.

CAROLINE. Well aren't you? So what were you an' her? Exactly like?

CHARLEY. Just randy right?

CAROLINE. You must have been right randy if she coming back to you after all these years! Come on what were you? Proper boyfriend girlfriend like? How long? . . . You were weren't you?! . . . Were it serious? . . . You know? Yeah? . . . Yeah?

CHARLEY. Aye. We were randy for each other.

CAROLINE. That isn't what I mean an' you know –

CHARLEY. God Caroline what is this? We were randy for each other, sometimes back then that were all you could hope for, not like now wi' you all playing the field like like some chuffing game for fucking perfection!

CAROLINE. I don't play the field . . . did you love her? I really wanna know.

CHARLEY. . . . We were having a baby.

CAROLINE. . . . Oh . . . oh . . . that isn't an answer.

CHARLEY. It only one I got.

CAROLINE. You never mentioned no kids.

CHARLEY. Well she died.

CAROLINE. She?

CHARLEY. Tracey.

CAROLINE. Tracey? How old were Tracey?

CHARLEY. Few month.

CAROLINE. . . . Soz . . . what she die of?

CHARLEY. Got pneumonia . . . . . . Connie, I were just randy for her.

CAROLINE. You didn't want the baby?

CHARLEY. No.

CAROLINE. Did she?

CHARLEY. I dunno. She were just randy for me. She were gonna be a teacher, or something.

CAROLINE. I'm gonna be a teacher.

CHARLEY. No, that's what you've told Richard you'll be to shut him up.

CAROLINE. Oh aye. She were gonna be a teacher then?

CHARLEY. Aye.

CAROLINE. But, if you didn't want it, couldn't you, you know?

CHARLEY. It weren't legal.

CAROLINE. You stuck with it?

CHARLEY. No. You could go see someone an' have it done.

CAROLINE. But you said it weren't legal.

CHARLEY. No it weren't.

CAROLINE. So what you mean?

CHARLEY. What you think I mean?

CAROLINE. I don't know.

CHARLEY. You'd go see this person when you're a bit gone an' they'd set you off.

CAROLINE. Set you off?

CHARLEY. An' you'd deliver what left.

CAROLINE. God.

CHARLEY. Both sets of parents agreed like too, right bollocksing you never heard likes of, but we all agreed, get rid. Didn't help that her folks were right snobby bastards. They all sorted the money out between 'em . . . she were so scared, of it hurting, killing, I never seen no girl so terrified. She begged me. She only seventeen, she begging me. Her folks said get rid or marry. So I married her.

CAROLINE. You married cos of the bairn?

CHARLEY. Them backstreet abortionists, they did alright out of it you know, there were some pennies to be made out of that game.

CAROLINE. You what?

CHARLEY. Them back street abortionists, their get rid jobs. It were like with all them tower blocks they building then. With the music an' clothes, folk getting randy . . . a growth industry . . .

CAROLINE. I only say about Connie cos after me and Richard gone you be here on yer own.

CHARLEY. There be new staff.

CAROLINE. I don't mean like that – god – you know what I mean. Me an' him, we been here five year, not five minute. We almost family.

CHARLEY. Richard?

CAROLINE. Well me yeah?

CHARLEY. I be alright.

CAROLINE. Tell me ought you.

CHARLEY. Aye.

CAROLINE. . . . So what this one about? One you been listening to?

CHARLEY. Nought.

CAROLINE. Think I heard you have this one on before. What's princess going on about?

CHARLEY. Princess?

CAROLINE. They always princesses in these things. You don't get bloody peasants singing like that do you?

CHARLEY. She isn't a princess, she a queen.

CAROLINE. That even worse. What's Queen going on about then?

CHARLEY. She's falling in love. An' her prince has a destiny.

CAROLINE. King. Her King.

CHARLEY. No, her he's a prince.

CAROLINE. Oh. There's always a prince. An' a destiny.

CHARLEY. Aye, an' prince's love for her don't fit in with his grand destiny.

CAROLINE. So what were that bit you listening to about? Sounded nice.

CHARLEY. Her prince leaves her, because she tells him to, because of his destiny, but she's so in love she can't go on, an' she wants forgiveness.

CAROLINE. What for?

CHARLEY. For being so in love she dies.

CAROLINE. Sounds silly.

CHARLEY. It is silly, to be so much in love.

CAROLINE. Is it?

CAROLINE looks at watch.

Bastard! Me break's done.

CHARLEY *takes CD out of player and starts to hurriedly pack away as if invaded. Thinking about it a moment* CAROLINE *takes the CD from him.*

CAROLINE. I'll listen to yer silly Queen if you don't mind?

CHARLEY. You don't have to.

CAROLINE. I want to. It'll be different. I like things that are different.

CHARLEY. No one's borrowed me music before.

CAROLINE. Then that's different for you an' all isn't it? Eh? . . . Well what do you think I'm gonna do to it?

CHARLEY. I don't know.

CAROLINE. . . . I gotta go.

CHARLEY *goes back to his packing.* CAROLINE *leaves, putting CD in her hung-up jacket as she passes it.*

Scene Four

Late into the evening. The pub has closed. The storeroom door opens and CAROLINE *and* RICHARD *enter rearranging the last bits of their clothes. They've just had sex in there.* CAROLINE *sits on the table,* RICHARD *loiters around the kitchen. He's a bit pissed.*

RICHARD. Right. I be back off down pool hall then.

CAROLINE. Yeah.

RICHARD. What you doing?

CAROLINE. Got essay on potato famine to finish.

RICHARD. Lovely. Sure you don't wanna come play pool?

CAROLINE. Yes.

RICHARD. Yes you do?

CAROLINE. Yes I'm sure I don't.

RICHARD. Right, I be off then.

CAROLINE. You gonna get pissed?

RICHARD. No. Promise . . . you got me on a string you know.

CAROLINE. We're both on a string.

RICHARD. I'm gonna miss that storeroom. Think aye, new place'll have a bed, bed that doesn't set ceiling off creaking. Bed we can shag in. Bed be great. It all be great. They say we all conform in the end.

CAROLINE. What end? I conformed at fifteen. My rebellious phase were the ninety second it took to shag you under age.

RICHARD. Not my fault. You said you eighteen. Still miss the uniform.

CAROLINE. Richard, that's six years ago. It's getting real pervy now.

RICHARD. Only cos it's you.

CAROLINE. Yeah well, I don't like it. I'm not yer school girl.

RICHARD. Didn't say you were.

CAROLINE. What's wrong wi' me waitress gear? Don't that do it for you?

RICHARD. But you always a waitress, it me bread and butter.

CAROLINE. I still be in pub waitressing even at uni.

RICHARD. Aye. You know a storeroom is other people's fantasy?

CAROLINE. Dunno why.

RICHARD. It's still my fantasy. I have you in the storeroom. You're me one an' fucking only.

CAROLINE. Aye.

RICHARD. My life weren't worth fucking ought 'fore you.

CAROLINE. I know.

RICHARD. Only time I been ought is . . . what?

CAROLINE. How much have you had?

RICHARD. Have you stopped being on the pill yet?

CAROLINE. I've said no.

RICHARD. No you have or no you . . . well even if you are still on it –

CAROLINE. I am!

RICHARD. Even if you are it's only ninety-nine times out of a hundred or something. I can beat them fucking odds.

CAROLINE. Richard shurrup.

RICHARD. Soz, sorry. You're not are you? It's cos we standing up, at funny angles like. It is.

CAROLINE. Richard. I don't want a baby.

RICHARD. You said you would. Now like.

CAROLINE. You what?

RICHARD. You did.

CAROLINE. When?

RICHARD. First year we were going out, first getting it on you said in four five year you'd like a bairn . . . which is now like!

CAROLINE. No.

RICHARD. You did.

CAROLINE. I'm sure I did but it isn't a fucking contract in blood or ought is it? I don't want one.

RICHARD. But it's fucking embarrassing.

CAROLINE. For who?

RICHARD. For me! It were me who announced we were trying for a family eighteen month ago like.

CAROLINE. No one's remembered you saying that cos you said it when you pissed.

RICHARD. And what's the fucking result? Huh? Nought. You on the pill aren't you?

CAROLINE. Well course I am. You know I am.

RICHARD. I'm happy to go for tests, not happy but I'll go.

CAROLINE. Richard for . . .

RICHARD. I'll go for tests – oh no, if you on pill, stupid.

CAROLINE. What's wrong with waiting?

RICHARD. How long then?

CAROLINE. I dunno.

RICHARD. Roughly.

CAROLINE. I dunno. Four, five, six, seven, eight years like . . . yeah?

RICHARD. Right but, I'm twenty-seven now.

CAROLINE. Yeah.

RICHARD. Well if I want grandchildren by time I'm in me fifties I –

CAROLINE. What the fuck are you going on about? For god's sake listen to yerself!

RICHARD. What?

CAROLINE. Just listen to yerself.

RICHARD. I don't understand. What do you want then?

CAROLINE. Nought, I want nought. Have you heard on yer transfer yet?

RICHARD. I would have told you wouldn't I? Every time phone goes I'm on edge. I can't be doing with it. An' I can't be doing with you at uni an' me here. God no. I'll get it. Get you transfer an'all.

CAROLINE. You have got your transfer.

RICHARD. But as landlord. And landlady. We haven't got that yet.

CAROLINE. I'm a waitress. I'm not your landlady.

RICHARD. You will. Me own gaffe. Landlord like. Be fucking amazing having name 'bove the door. It be so great. Miles away though is Bradford. God, it so far.

CAROLINE. Aye.

RICHARD. Long way from me Mam . . . I best be off down pool hall, get practice in.

CAROLINE. For what?

RICHARD. Well in me new gaffe near yer uni we'll have a big fuck off pool table so I can thrash all yer uni mates won't I?

CAROLINE. Will you?

RICHARD. Oh aye. I might not have grades or big fuck off I.T. salaries but I thrash 'em at fucking pool. Specially ones that fall in love with yer.

CAROLINE. Wi' me?

RICHARD. Aye. There will, there be some soppy saft as piss water eighteen, nineteen year olds with dicks sticking outta their trousers fancying their chances with you, thinking they love you, you being older woman an' all.

CAROLINE. Me? Older woman?

RICHARD. You're twenty-one, you be all woman to these eighteen-year-olds, not all girl like you were to me. You be a right Mrs Robinson to 'em wi' the whole mature student thing you got going on there.

CAROLINE. . . . Nah.

RICHARD. Yeah – you mature you. Old.

CAROLINE. Am I?

RICHARD. You not gonna leave me are you?

CAROLINE. What you like?

RICHARD. I mean for some saft as piss water student? I almost wish you would. I mean it isn't like it were when we first got it on in club and first year or so like is it? We can be honest about that can't we?

CAROLINE. Aye.

RICHARD. We gotta keep going forward Caroline. Like you're meant to do.

CAROLINE. Like what?

RICHARD. We should have got married by now. Few year back like. We could have had right do and spread in here. Charley'd have done us a right good sit down meal an' buffet. I like a good buffet.

CAROLINE. We don't need to be married to be happy.

RICHARD. No, it not 'bout that. Married is saying even when you not happy you gonna be together. It saying you gonna be fucking miserable together but you still together. You put your lives together. It a show of trust, all legal like, what mine is yours, fifty fifty an' all that.

CAROLINE. What we got isn't worth –

RICHARD. It idea of it though. It an idea. I am you, you are me and we are . . . you know.

CAROLINE. Yeah.

RICHARD. There has to be a journey hasn't there? Can't stay same like.

CAROLINE. We not though, we off to uni. Be together. Be all different.

RICHARD. That not what I mean an' you know it. There I be same like . . . look, if you think you'll meet someone else, just say. Yeah?

CAROLINE. But I love you you git.

RICHARD. You just can't bear being on yer own.

CAROLINE. No. I do love you.

RICHARD. It isn't enough. It isn't legal like. It isn't ought like. It just words.

CAROLINE. No matter how much you in love wi' someone, how happy like you are, life, it makes everything, ought into just routine. Routine fucking bludgeons everything it does. Doesn't it? Even me an' you.

RICHARD. Aye! So we mix it up aye? Marry? Trust.

CAROLINE. But I do trust you.

RICHARD. I'll go have a fucking affair.

CAROLINE. Go on then.

RICHARD. Well kids then, yeah? You still do yer uni. An' kids, always changing they are, always. Live through 'em you do. Every few year they totally different, like a constant shot in the arm they are . . . you want to do it on table? Like we used to when we first met? Be like old times' sake. You want to? I mean it's your bum not mine.

CAROLINE. Why's it have to be my bum?

RICHARD. Health n' safety go crazy they saw that, not putting me bare bum on it.

CAROLINE. What you wanna go again for?

RICHARD. Cos.

CAROLINE. Well you'll have to be quick, I no time for – I got an essay on the potato famine to do.

RICHARD. God. You'll have to gimme a mo. Gimme a hand?

CAROLINE. Richard –

RICHARD. Well you'll have to if you wanna go again.

CAROLINE. But I don't.

RICHARD. But I do.

CAROLINE. Oh for fuck's sake!

RICHARD *leaves, off down veranda steps.*

CAROLINE *sits on table and tries to compose herself. Then she makes to leave out through bar but stops by her hung-up jacket, she takes out the CD and puts it in player. She sits, smokes and listens.*

Scene Five

Morning.

RICHARD *is lying asleep out on the veranda, pissed.*
CAROLINE *enters from bar in dressing gown.*

CAROLINE. Richard? Richard?

She sees him out on the veranda and kneels beside him.
CHARLEY *enters ready for shift, hanging stuff up as usual. Sees them on veranda.*

CHARLEY. Is he pissed?

CAROLINE. Aye. He said wouldn't. He promised.

CHARLEY. Chuffing odds on if he promises.

CAROLINE. Aye . . . he didn't mean to.

CHARLEY. I best go get veg in.

CAROLINE *stays sat beside* RICHARD. CHARLEY *tries to busy himself as* CONNIE *enters from bar, just arrived, takes coat and stuff off. Sees* CAROLINE *on veranda and goes to say hello. Sees* RICHARD.

CONNIE. . . . Hello.

CAROLINE. Hiya. Don't worry, he's alright. He just pissed.

CONNIE *goes back into the kitchen to find something to do which embarrasses* CAROLINE.

CONNIE. Is she embarrassed?

CHARLEY. Aye.

CONNIE. Hopefully I'll be better today.

CHARLEY. You did alright yesterday.

CONNIE. I don't know how you do it.

CHARLEY. Just do. Don't know why you're doing it . . . good chance of rain today. Make it not so manic.

CONNIE. Yes.

CHARLEY. You were thrown in the deep end yesterday.

CONNIE. Right.

CHARLEY *goes back to some work.*

Charley?

CHARLEY. Yes?

CONNIE. What shall I do? . . . Work, I mean . . .

CHARLEY. Yes.

CONNIE. If he's drunk, aren't you in charge? Of me?

CHARLEY. Aye.

CONNIE. I'll scrub the table?

CHARLEY. It doesn't need doing.

CONNIE. Right. There must be something.

CHARLEY. Aye. I got to go get the veg in, he's pissed. I must go get veg. I think of something.

CHARLEY *leaves by bar door.* CONNIE *just stands there, waiting.*

CAROLINE *is nudging* RICHARD *who stirs, wakes looking at* CAROLINE.

RICHARD. Caroline?

CAROLINE. Yeah?

RICHARD. What's time?

CAROLINE. Nearly opening. Ray'll be –

RICHARD. Best get coffee on then.

CAROLINE. What you got like this for?

RICHARD. Practice!

CAROLINE. For what?

RICHARD. To thrash yer fucking uni mates. Six pints an' rest an' I still getting them balls down them holes, good that isn't it? I'm at me fucking prime me.

CAROLINE. Yeah great, come on.

RICHARD. I'll drink your fucking uni mates under table! Ey! Know what I can do?

CAROLINE. Richard we no time for this.

RICHARD. No know what I can do?

CAROLINE. What?

RICHARD. If you pissed sleeping on floor you can think yer head's where yer tum is an' it like a pillow – fucking good that.

CAROLINE. Aye great, come on, up, now!

CAROLINE helps RICHARD to his feet. CHARLEY enters from bar door carrying boxes of veg he puts in storeroom and comes back out into the kitchen as CAROLINE helps RICHARD in, sitting him face down at the table. CHARLEY makes to go to the kettle.

No Charley, you leave that you just worry 'bout food alright?

CHARLEY. Just helping.

CAROLINE. I know you were but I don't want you getting bollocking –

CHARLEY. Don't bother me.

CAROLINE. Charley! I haven't time for this!

CHARLEY. Sorry love.

CAROLINE fusses about getting pot of coffee on.

Ray be down soon.

CAROLINE. Charley I fucking know! . . . Sorry.

RICHARD. Bloody hell Charley.

CAROLINE. Oh god.

RICHARD. You in early aren't you?

CHARLEY. It you in late.

SCENE FIVE   43

RICHARD. Am I?

CHARLEY. Aye.

RICHARD. Well fucking chuffa nora then! You not bloody done ought have you? An' what she doing? She not bloody doing ought is she? Connie!

CONNIE. Yes?

RICHARD. There be bit of cheese in that fridge there.

CONNIE. Yes?

RICHARD. Grate it!

CONNIE. Right.

CONNIE goes to the fridge and brings out a big block of cheese which needs two hands to lift. She puts it on table, trying to work out what to do with it throughout the following.

RICHARD. An' you?

CHARLEY. Aye?

RICHARD. Just . . . just get it sorted will you?

CAROLINE. Richard.

RICHARD. . . . Oh no no no no no!

CHARLEY. What?

RICHARD. Oh dear me, I nearly put me fucking foot in it. Bugger. I'm not to bollock you.

CHARLEY. Aren't you?

RICHARD. No, cos, cos –

CHARLEY. Cos?

RICHARD. My Caroline. You see' don't tell no one – but you like Connie.

CHARLEY. Right.

RICHARD. Aye! My Caroline says an' yeah, she right. I'm not to bollock you you know. Cos Connie, you like her an'

I haven't have I? Part from just now nearly. So Charley has Connie come round to yer charms yet then?

RICHARD *winks and clicks his tongue at* CONNIE.

Cos, cos my Caroline, she feeling she . . . she could bring north an' south poles together. She wanting people to be in love like, like they are at start when it all phwoarh an' everything! Do you still get that when you old codgers?

CAROLINE. Richard will you shut up!

RICHARD. Ey ey ey, I'm just –

CAROLINE. No you're not. Go on.

RICHARD. No but I haven't bollocksed him now have I?

CAROLINE. No.

RICHARD. So I kept my side of bargain like, so a baby right? Four years? Four years from now and counting? A bairn?

CAROLINE. If I say yes will you get in shower?

RICHARD. Aye.

CAROLINE. Alright. Now go on. Please.

RICHARD. Hello Connie.

CONNIE. Hello Richard.

RICHARD. Just think of it Connie.

CAROLINE. Richard! Shhurrup 'bout bairns. Shower!

RICHARD. Connie think of it, everytime in here he squeezes past you, phwoarh!

RICHARD *slaps and rubs his belly.*

Wobble wobble wobble.

CAROLINE. Shut up!

RICHARD. Phwoarh! . . . I bagsy shower.

RICHARD *stumbles out.*

CHARLEY. If he could just overcome his shyness . . .

CAROLINE. Yeah. I best do sauces or something hadn't I?

CHARLEY. Aye.

CAROLINE. I'm sorry . . . I listened to all of it you know.

CHARLEY. What?

CAROLINE. Yer music . . . I liked it . . . I loved it . . . you gonna say ought?

CHARLEY. . . . I'm glad you like it.

CAROLINE. Yeah . . . I loved it. It repeats itself right lot but words are all printed in booklet aren't they?

CHARLEY. Aye.

CAROLINE. So you can follow it back an' forth like an . . . yeah.

CAROLINE gets box of sauces from storeroom and goes into the bar. CHARLEY watches CONNIE struggling with the cheese.

CHARLEY. Con . . .

CONNIE. Yes?

CHARLEY. You don't have to grate all of it.

CHARLEY helps CONNIE.

Scene Six

Early evening. CHARLEY is tidying up for the day, packs away music, dithers a few moments about whether to leave CD behind/in player – he leaves it.

CONNIE. Caroline listens to your music?

CHARLEY. Aye.

CONNIE. What she doing that for? Young girl like her?

CHARLEY. She must like it.

CONNIE. . . . It didn't rain.

CHARLEY. Never does when they say it will.

CONNIE. I did better today didn't I?

CHARLEY. Aye.

CONNIE. I wasn't very fast, but I was better.

CHARLEY. You were fast enough.

CONNIE. I know you won't believe me, but I rather like it here.

CHARLEY. Do you?

CONNIE. Yes. Busy. Rush. Can't think. Busy. I like it.

CHARLEY. It only cos it summer, it won't be manic forever.

CONNIE. But when it isn't I still get a few hours here and there won't I?

CHARLEY. Oh aye, I expect so. They work something out.

CONNIE. It mine this. Aye, an' when Richard an' Caroline leave I be one showing new people this an' that, how to do a few things. Won't I?

CHARLEY. Suppose so.

CONNIE. You leaving her the music to listen to?

CHARLEY. Aye. She said she likes it.

CONNIE. She did. You'll miss her?

CHARLEY. Aye.

> CHARLEY *goes back to his packing.* CONNIE *goes out onto veranda, looking out. This disturbs* CHARLEY, *he stands in doorway looking at her.*

What you doing there?

CONNIE. Nothing.

CHARLEY. You can't stand there an' say you doing nothing.

CONNIE. Why?

CHARLEY. You know why.

CONNIE. I used to wait for you here on an evening, whilst you finished up, before going for a ride.

CHARLEY. Aye.

CONNIE. It hasn't changed.

CHARLEY. What you expect it to do?

CONNIE. Don't know. The view has. More houses. Less green.

CHARLEY. Aye.

CONNIE. It were more countryside then. Round here, you couldn't ride your bike round here now like you did then.

CHARLEY. No I couldn't.

CONNIE. My folks hated that bike. Soon as they saw it that were it – hated you. Mind you, if one of my girls had brought likes of you home on a bike like that, I wouldn't have been happy would have been putting it mildly, my David would have gone – oh aye, I can see where me folks were coming from . . . but I loved that bike. You could go so fast, turn corners so fast –

CHARLEY. I fell off in the end.

CONNIE. I thought I'd fall off.

CHARLEY. Aye.

CONNIE. But I never did. An' then I'd go in yer ear faster Charley faster faster.

CHARLEY. Stupid.

CONNIE. Aye. Dangerous an' all.

CHARLEY. Very.

CONNIE. . . . It were good though.

CHARLEY. Aye.

CONNIE. Good this time of year too when it were light so late, stay out for ages . . . it hasn't changed so much . . . my parents are both dead you know. There's no one from then who knows I'm here. There's no one who wasn't keen on you, you know. There's just me and you . . . do you understand?

CHARLEY. . . . Aye.

CONNIE. Do you? . . . You understand why they weren't keen on you?

CHARLEY. Yob on a bike aye.

CONNIE. And the rest?

CHARLEY. Work in here an' marrying you? Aye, it isn't rocket science.

CONNIE. No.

CHARLEY. No, me marrying you, right bollocksed their plans up. Aye. Right bastard me. Worth doing just to see look on their faces . . . sorry. I didn't, I didn't mean that.

CONNIE. You still hate them?

CHARLEY. Saying get rid or marry? Least wi' my folks you knew where you stood. All marriage meant to them were chance of a dinner an' a knees up.

CONNIE. There were no knees up at our wedding.

CHARLEY. No there weren't.

CONNIE. Least your folks, they didn't criticise so much.

CHARLEY. Not so much.

CONNIE. And they were happy weren't they? For us?

CHARLEY. Oh aye they were, bless 'em.

CONNIE. They thought marriage'd calm you down, get you off that bike at least. Least yours could see some good in it. I liked them.

CHARLEY. . . . You like a drink? I'd like a drink. We could sit out here I suppose?

SCENE SIX   49

CONNIE *nods. He gets drinks, they sit out on crates on veranda.*

CONNIE. My folks were right in a way, about you.

CHARLEY. You what?

CONNIE. They said you'd never do anything. An' you never.

CHARLEY. Wouldn't want to be disappointing them.

CONNIE. You used to sit in here on an evening when we were first courting an' you were saying how you'd like to go travelling . . . you never even moved to the city, not London, not even Leeds. For years after when I were married to David I were expecting you to just go one day. Just disappear an' I'd hear from someone how you'd gone, an' I'd never know where. An' I could imagine like, somewhere like, but you never . . . you said you'd go, take me with you you said.

CHARLEY. I said lots of things.

CONNIE. I believed you.

CHARLEY. You didn't want to do that.

CONNIE. When we were expecting Tracey you'd sit in here on an evening or we'd go up moors and you'd say how we'd go to Australia, get away from them, an' their criticising. Am I remembering right, when Tracey were born, we were going?

CHARLEY. Maybe.

CONNIE. Did we make any plans?

CHARLEY. Few inquiries. Nought booked.

CONNIE. You ever been?

CHARLEY. No. You?

CONNIE. David took me. In 1980 for a month. It's nice. Me an' you were just gonna go weren't we? You could then. You can't now.

CHARLEY. Can't you?

CONNIE. My youngest tried to go a few year back. You have to be under twenty-six or twenty-seven and prove you are some benefit to the economy.

CHARLEY. Bugger . . . good thing now wasn't then then?

CONNIE. But we'd never have had Tracey if then was now. Wouldn't have been thinking of getting away.

CHARLEY. What would we have been?

CONNIE. Just . . . randy, I suppose.

CHARLEY. Aye. Few year later, when you heard it were legal, what did you think?

CONNIE. I cried.

CHARLEY. Who for? . . . Did your David know about your flowers?

CONNIE. Yes.

CHARLEY. An' he were happy with you doing them?

CONNIE. He never said ought.

CHARLEY. Said what?

CONNIE. Anything.

CHARLEY. But he let you?

CONNIE. Aye.

CHARLEY. Well, they're for the bairn.

CONNIE. I wasn't in love with him you know . . . ever.

CHARLEY. Connie?

CONNIE. I wasn't.

CHARLEY. Did he know that?

CONNIE. Yes.

CHARLEY. How?

CONNIE. A few year ago, he just said he'd always known, because he said, you just do. After the girls all left home, I was going to leave him.

SCENE SIX 51

CHARLEY. But you never.

CONNIE. From age of nineteen he's all I known.

CHARLEY. Why'd you marry him then?

CONNIE. He said he loved me.

CHARLEY. Did he?

CONNIE. Aye, an' I believed him. He wanted a family. I wanted a family. Something to love, unconditional . . .

CHARLEY. You didn't?

CONNIE. He was kind, an' he was lovely, yes.

CHARLEY. But . . .

CONNIE. Maybe that's why we lasted, cos if I was never in love with him he couldn't hurt me could he? After the girls had gone I did try to make it work, there were phases like, convince myself but, but me girls kept coming back visiting with their lives, their futures an' their husbands that they're in love with, an' I . . . I wanted that – what I'd given them . . . after Tracey I were waiting for you to go. Me folks were, we all were, me folks couldn't wait for you to . . . they said you a coward trying to make out you loved me . . . thought I'd make it easy for you, an' go. I mean I only had Tracey cos I so frightened of having it done . . . I didn't want her. No one wanted me baby.

CHARLEY. Last time I tried to speak to you 'fore you left, you were sat in bath an' water going right cold, an' you sat in it you daft – I tried to get you out . . . you wouldn't let me touch you. An' I still put me arm round you, comfort you, you cried like I disgusted you. Like you wanted me to hear you cry.

CONNIE. You said you loved me.

CHARLEY. Well what you meant to say?

CONNIE. I know. I know. An' yes, it were nice of you to say, make out you . . . that would have been fine in a way, no problem . . . problem is, I were so in love with you. That the problem.

CHARLEY. Loved me?

CONNIE. Aye.

CHARLEY. But you wouldn't let me near you.

CONNIE. I know.

CHARLEY. You . . . you didn't say ought to me 'bout loving me.

CONNIE. Well not that I could could I? We could all see you felt so miserable an' trapped by the whole thing, you only married me cos of the bairn, last thing you need were me, some daft girl you just randy for saying she loved you. You were being so nice and good to me, I loved you, I weren't telling you I loved you, weren't doing that to you.

CHARLEY. But you didn't say . . .

CONNIE. I remember our wedding day, I were so in love with you, yet I felt so miserable.

CHARLEY. You still feel . . . ?

CONNIE. Could we be friends?

CHARLEY. Friends?

CONNIE. Aye.

CHARLEY. Do you still, feel, you know?

CONNIE. Yes. I do.

CHARLEY. We best be friends then.

They sit there.

Scene Seven

Later that evening. Pub in full flow.

CHARLEY *is sat out on veranda listening to some music wafting out of the kitchen. It finishes as* CAROLINE *enters and lingers in the veranda doorway.*

CAROLINE. You still here?

CHARLEY. What time is it?

CAROLINE. Getting on. Be last orders soon. Connie stayed a while? You talked?

CHARLEY. Aye.

CAROLINE. I'm pleased. I'm right to be pleased? You need a friend. You want a fag?

CHARLEY. No ta.

CAROLINE. Go on.

CHARLEY. No thanks.

CAROLINE. Please.

CHARLEY. Caroline what is this?

CAROLINE. Nought, you want a fag?

CHARLEY. Why?

CAROLINE. . . . Dunno. Cos.

CHARLEY. Why cos? . . .

CAROLINE. . . . Cos.

CHARLEY. Caroline, if I'm only one you can talk to . . .

CAROLINE. Yeah?

CHARLEY. You should change that.

She holds fag out to him. He takes it, she lights it for him.

Where'd you rush off in yer lunch break?

CAROLINE. To find him, to talk.

CHARLEY. You shouldn't have done that.

CAROLINE. Why?

CHARLEY. Gone running.

CAROLINE. I didn't.

CHARLEY. You did. He played you, knew how to make you go running.

CAROLINE. It didn't take long. I went everywhere I could think of, pool hall an' his Mam's.

CHARLEY. Pool hall?

CAROLINE. No his Mam's. So we couldn't talk there anyway, had to be all smiles like . . . Yer music, bit near start, where she falls right in love wi' her prince, tune an' everything it uses, that good isn't it?

CHARLEY. Aye it is.

CAROLINE. Course she's stupid. Queen like.

CHARLEY. She is.

CAROLINE. Falling in love like that, throwing all buggery to the wind.

CHARLEY. Oh.

CAROLINE. She is. But what we all really wanna do isn't it? How she feels at the end, when she dies cos she's too much in love, you know I never felt ought like that . . . when I were fifteen an' me Mam an' Dad were splitting, Richard were so great, I mean when they split he were me everything, me one an' fucking only . . . but, I reckon I just wanted to have feelings for someone, maybe it didn't matter who . . . so I turned up on his doorstep here wi' me stuff.

CHARLEY. I remember.

CAROLINE. He couldn't believe it.

CHARLEY. No, he couldn't.

CAROLINE. Never meant to stay, just get me head together but, we were happy, and I had these feelings, he was cute . . . that Queen dying like that, never felt ought like, those feelings right good, sad, but beautiful. She well fucked herself didn't she . . . soz, that's him talking.

CHARLEY. No . . . haven't you got an essay or something to do?

CAROLINE. Aye. I have.

CHARLEY. Shouldn't you be getting on with it?

CAROLINE. Don't you wanna talk about yer music?

CHARLEY. I never talked to no one about me music.

CAROLINE. More reason to then, wouldn't you like to?

CHARLEY. It private.

CAROLINE. But I've heard it, I know what it's about, what it makes you feel.

CHARLEY. Caroline, what's up?

CAROLINE. . . . I've had the phonecall. About his transfer.

CHARLEY. It not his own pub?

CAROLINE. Nah. Course it isn't.

CHARLEY. No.

CAROLINE. No.

CHARLEY. What's he said?

CAROLINE. I haven't said.

CHARLEY. Caroline.

CAROLINE. I will.

CHARLEY. Well where is he?

CAROLINE. Down pool hall.

CHARLEY. I meant where in the new pub?

CAROLINE. Same as here. Kitchen like. Well, no like about it, it is kitchen . . . maybe I won't go to Bradford. I could still apply an' try for elsewhere I bet, give him chance to apply somewhere he do bit better.

CHARLEY. No you're not.

CAROLINE. I could.

CHARLEY. But you're not. You only even going to Bradford cos he don't want to go too far. Chuffing Bradford.

CAROLINE. Charley.

CHARLEY. Get him told.

CAROLINE. I don't know.

CHARLEY. Well marry him then.

CAROLINE. I don't wanna.

CHARLEY. Get up duff to him.

CAROLINE. I don't want to. I'm not going to.

CHARLEY. Well then . . .

CAROLINE. But I need him . . . did you want to marry Connie?

CHARLEY. I did marry her.

CAROLINE. That not what I asked.

CHARLEY. I had to.

CAROLINE. Aye, but why?

CHARLEY. Cos I had to.

CAROLINE. I could have a bairn wi' Richard now an' no one give a shit. Could have years ago, no one give a shit then, almost expected of me it were then. I could marry him, don't mean chuffing ought, wouldn't even get him less tax to pay, there no chuffing point. It just saying we in love, we happy, we "we." An' I know that, don't need no ceremony in eyes of god or law or ought to tell me that I know that, an' feel . . .

CHARLEY. What?

CAROLINE. I'm lonely, an' I have to pretend I'm not. I love him, but I don't feel ought, cos this Queen, she makes you feel stuff doesn't she? You can't help yourself feeling stuff. That what I don't understand, how can you listen to that, and you be you? Cos I can't.

CHARLEY. I'm glad you like it. You must get him told.

CAROLINE. I'll say to him soon as he gets back.

CHARLEY. Say what?

CAROLINE. . . . Not gonna get me essay done am I?

CHARLEY. I should be getting off.

CHARLEY gathers his stuff together.

CAROLINE. You ever listened to this with someone?

CAROLINE turns the music on. CHARLEY sits back down, CAROLINE lights him a fag. They listen.

. . . time passes to later in the evening, darker. CHARLEY has gone. It is later in the opera, CAROLINE still listening as RICHARD enters up veranda steps. She realises he is there and switches the music off, wipes her eyes, stands there innocent.

RICHARD. What you doing?

CAROLINE. Nought.

RICHARD. You no college stuff doing?

CAROLINE. No.

RICHARD comes up to her giving her a cuddle.

RICHARD. You've got tears. The lights catching 'em . . .

CAROLINE. It isn't.

RICHARD. Then what you wiping yer eyes for? Them tears. I'm so soz I bollocked him. I were a right bastard this morning. I hate myself for it you know. When you were round at me Mam's I wanted to say but we had to be all happy faces like. Me an' you, we good at happy faces. I haven't meant to be like I been.

CAROLINE. No you're alright. It's this.

RICHARD. What?

CAROLINE. It were this.

CHARLEY. Charley's shite?

CAROLINE. Aye.

CAROLINE motions to the player.

RICHARD. But it shite that.

CAROLINE. There's one of his on here, all of it's good an' different like but, this one, it's good . . . beautiful.

RICHARD. I thought he were still here, sad bastard.

CAROLINE. No, it's me.

RICHARD. We hate Charley's shite.

CAROLINE. Well, apart from this one. It's sad.

RICHARD. What you gotta be sad about?

CAROLINE. Nought.

RICHARD. Then what you crying for?

CAROLINE. I'm not.

RICHARD. You are. Tell me.

CAROLINE. It's about a prince an' princess – a queen, falling in love 'til she's too much in love, that's all.

RICHARD. That's . . .

CAROLINE. Aye – shite. I know.

RICHARD. I thought it was to you . . . why'd you turn it off?

CAROLINE. Cos you don't like it . . . yer transfer's come through. I had a call.

RICHARD. Oh right, it . . .

CAROLINE. Yeah.

RICHARD. It isn't me own pub, is it?

CAROLINE. No.

RICHARD. No it is or no it isn't?

CAROLINE. It isn't.

RICHARD. Who are they putting in?

CAROLINE. Some temporary people we'll be sharing with.

RICHARD. Where am I?

CAROLINE. You're in the kitchen.

RICHARD. Right . . . I don't mind you know, for all me cock an' bull bluster I were expecting it.

CAROLINE. I know.

RICHARD. Just, why'd I have to hear it from you ey?

CAROLINE. You alright?

RICHARD *kisses her, takes her hand leading her towards storeroom.*

No I –

RICHARD. What? . . . you rather stay an' listen to that shite?

CAROLINE *gives in letting* RICHARD *lead her into the storeroom, door closes behind them.*

Scene Eight

Morning.

CHARLEY *has recently arrived for work. Getting on with some preparation work.* CONNIE *arrives carrying a bunch of flowers, a posey, the kind of flowers she puts on the grave.*

CONNIE. I been to do my flowers. They were going off. Yours weren't. You never let yours go off. Maybe we could go put some on together. We never have, don't you think we should? . . . You alright?

CHARLEY. Fine Connie, fine.

CONNIE. You think it rain today?

CHARLEY. No, it be manic.

CONNIE *holds onto her flowers a moment and then puts them down on table as* RICHARD *enters, hungover, rough looking. Starts to make a coffee. As following happens* CONNIE *gets on with work, getting noticeably better at it, bit more gusto and confidence about her – but forgetting about the flowers.*

RICHARD. Aye aye alright. Don't start or ought.

CHARLEY. We open in minute.

RICHARD. I chuffing know . . .

CHARLEY. You got time for that?

RICHARD. I'm making the chuffing time.

CHARLEY. Going to be manic . . . Richard.

RICHARD. Aye. Going to be crazy insane manic . . . Caroline about?

CHARLEY. She at college isn't she?

RICHARD. . . . Aye.

CHARLEY. Is she?

RICHARD. She chuffing is alright!

CHARLEY. Sorry . . .

RICHARD. What?

CHARLEY. Nothing, I'm sorry to hear about yer transfer.

RICHARD. She told you?

CHARLEY. I'm sorry.

RICHARD. Yeah well, get somewhere else.

CHARLEY. Yes she might.

RICHARD. What you mean?

CHARLEY. She thinking of going somewhere else, so you can apply again, for another transfer.

RICHARD. She say that?

CHARLEY. Aye.

RICHARD. Aye well, with her results, it could be a bit flexible like.

CHARLEY. . . . Aye, you going to let her?

RICHARD. Aye. Suppose.

CHARLEY. Where you thinking of going?

RICHARD. I don't chuffing know alright?

CHARLEY. Sorry.

Sees flowers on table.

RICHARD. Chuff's sake Charley! What I bloody say to you eh?

He picks flowers up and stuffs them in bin.

RICHARD. Come on, pair of you. Open in few minute, pick the pace up!

They go about their work. RICHARD *loses interest in the coffee and goes out onto the veranda and lights a comfort fag.* CONNIE *is buried in work.*

RICHARD *comes back into kitchen and goes to the CD player, opens it and sees the CD, closes it and flicks through a couple of Dido & Aeneas tracks – but can't find what he wants.*

CHARLEY. What you doing?

RICHARD. Nought.

CHARLEY. We open in few minute.

RICHARD *keeps looking.*

Richard?

RICHARD. Stop being a bairn. I won't break it.

CHARLEY. What you doing?

RICHARD. What's it look like I'm doing?

CHARLEY. Looks like you're listening to me shite.

RICHARD. Looks right then don't it?

CHARLEY. Two minute we open.

RICHARD. Sssshhh! Trying to listen.

CHARLEY. What you listening for?

> RICHARD *finds the lament and allows it to play.*

RICHARD. Ssshh! This is it. Aye. All simple like. Her singing, no choir an' orchestra.

- He turns it off.

It shite that. That not changed.

CHARLEY. No.

RICHARD. Take it home.

CHARLEY. What you saying?

RICHARD. I saying take it home.

CHARLEY. You saying she can't listen?

RICHARD. No I not, but take it home, like you always do.

CHARLEY. It only that one she listens to.

RICHARD. I don't care, I'm not coming in here an' finding her on her own listening to your shite upsetting her. She don't need it, she got exams to do an' she listening to your shite.

CHARLEY. . . . If she likes it –

RICHARD. Oh aye?

CHARLEY. What?

RICHARD. Aye? Aye?

CHARLEY. Richard what?

RICHARD. Fancy your chances do you?

CHARLEY. What?

RICHARD. You think she want your crusty hands poring her?

CHARLEY. . . . No.

RICHARD. You dirty bastard . . . oh come on mate, don't look so surprised, don't pretend it hadn't ever crossed yer mind.

CHARLEY. What hasn't?

RICHARD. Don't insult me intelligence here Charley. It Caroline! You know what I mean, not even for a sec like?

CHARLEY. No.

RICHARD. You off wi' fairies listening to yer music are you thinking what she might be like? I tell you mate, fucking fantastic in ways you can't even –

CHARLEY. No!

RICHARD. Even wi' yer workings all crusted up it gonna cross yer mind.

CHARLEY. You worried about me? Me? Look at me Richard, look at me. What you gonna be like when you get to her uni eh?

RICHARD. What you mean?

CHARLEY. You know what I mean.

RICHARD. I'll twat 'em.

The ticker goes.

CHARLEY. Richard. She weren't gonna stay fifteen forever now was she?

RICHARD. Kind of hoping she would. It only plan I got.

The ticker goes again. They look at it. RICHARD *just stands there.* CHARLEY *gets it and starts trying to prepare the order.* RICHARD *wanders back out onto veranda still smoking.*

CHARLEY. Richard!

The ticker goes again. RICHARD *finishes fag, calmly stubs it out and wanders off down the veranda steps, gone. The ticker goes again.*

CONNIE. I'll help you.

CHARLEY. I don't think of her like that.

CONNIE. Let's hope it rains.

CHARLEY. I don't.

CONNIE. I know you don't.

They start to prepare the orders.

Scene Nine

Early evening.

CHARLEY *and* CONNIE *quietly finishing up for the day.* RICHARD *sat out on veranda smoking.*

CAROLINE *enters from bar looking for* RICHARD *and wanders out onto the veranda.*

RICHARD. Caroline?

CAROLINE. . . . . What? Thought you'd be down pool hall by now.

RICHARD. No.

CAROLINE. Getting some practice in. I hear you were getting some right extra practice in today.

RICHARD. Aye.

CAROLINE. What that in aid of going off like that? Lucky Charley an' Connie covering you.

RICHARD. I had monk on. That all.

CAROLINE. You get another transfer. We go somewhere else, somehow.

RICHARD. Will we? . . . What you doing out here?

CAROLINE. Fag before me shift.

He lights her a fag.

RICHARD. How were college?

CAROLINE. Alright.

RICHARD. What'd you do?

CAROLINE. Practice papers.

RICHARD. You do good?

CAROLINE. Dunno.

RICHARD. Could do with yer in here tomorrow then.

CAROLINE. College comes first now.

RICHARD. . . . I'm sorry about me transfer.

CAROLINE. I'm sorry for you.

RICHARD. Aye. But it's right near your uni so that's good isn't it?

CAROLINE. Yeah.

RICHARD. An' alright. I'm still just fucking assistant but it should be right better room, no more shagging in storeroom 'fore closing, no creaking shit hole like, mean it will be a shit hole but can't be no more of one than here can it? An' you can have all shifts you like they say. That be good won't it?

CAROLINE. Aye.

RICHARD. I think so. We'll have right good laugh. Best laughs yet to come. Bet new gaffer does lock-ins and we'll have all your new uni mates in cos you and yer fella work there and I'll thrash 'em all at pool and watch they don't take advantage of free beer . . . aye, when I'm finished in kitchen I'll join you and yer uni mates getting pissed . . . ey?

RICHARD *leaves off down veranda steps.* CAROLINE *sits there, listening to the following* . . . CONNIE *finishes her work.*

CONNIE. You like a drink?

CHARLEY. No ta.

CONNIE. We could sit out on the veranda?

CHARLEY. Caroline's having a fag out there.

CONNIE. Oh . . . You think a lot of her though don't you?

CHARLEY. Do I?

CONNIE. Aye. She sticks up for you, listens to yer music now, an' she were bein' right nosey about me an' you. I think you mean a lot to her.

CHARLEY. Well, I known her since she were fifteen. She lives above shop so to speak. She almost family . . . just want her to be happy.

CONNIE. We could have a drink in here?

CHARLEY. No ta.

CONNIE. Charley, you sure everything alright?

CHARLEY. Aye, aye.

CONNIE. Okay, I not sure I believe that . . . see you tomorrow then?

CHARLEY. Aye aye . . . no.

CONNIE. No?

CHARLEY. No you right. Connie, it not right this.

CONNIE. What you mean?

CHARLEY. Having you here. You been in front of me all the time.

CONNIE. What's the matter?

CHARLEY. That. Bein' like familiar.

CONNIE. Oh, I don't know what I can do about that.

SCENE NINE   67

CHARLEY. Tomorrow, I don't want you to come back.

CONNIE. We're going to be friends, that's all.

CHARLEY. It not good for you, we're not going to be friends.

CONNIE. But we've been talking lovely. Richard and Caroline are going. You be on yer own.

CHARLEY. I don't know no different. I'm happy, don't bother me.

CONNIE. No. Well, I'm getting good at this, better, an' it mine this.

CHARLEY. Con no, you say you were in love wi' me, you wanna be friends wi' me, how can you be in here knowing I don't feel the same way? . . . It isn't good for you.

CONNIE. Well, you get used to things. Don't you?

CHARLEY. Aye. That you do.

CONNIE. I never stopped doing my flowers –

CHARLEY. They're for the bairn!

CONNIE. Alright alright . . .

CHARLEY. Mine are for the bairn, yours are for the bairn – they're always for the barin . . . Con, no more.

CONNIE. . . . Couldn't we be friends?

CHARLEY. Like have drinks now, chat now, laugh now, be happy now – you be wanting everything you could have had then now?

CONNIE. Yes.

CHARLEY. An' all reminding you what you could have had?

CONNIE. But just friends. That all I want. Wouldn't bother me.

CHARLEY. You're not gonna have it are you?

CONNIE. Why can't we be?

CHARLEY. I . . . I'm in love with you.

CONNIE. You what?

CHARLEY. Once Tracey were born. I were. Totally.

CONNIE. No.

CHARLEY. Aye. I think I were before, but I could never quite get it out, think it, feel it, there just weren't the words, the feelings an' stuff in me head for me get it out back then. So difficult. I just couldn't figure out how to say it to you, and make you believe it. Just words. An' I always thought right back when I were just randy for you what's this bright beautiful young thing doing wi' a greasy yob on a bike like me? Couldn't work it out, everything yer folks thought an' said, I'd thought it first.

CONNIE. Charley . . .

CHARLEY. Last time we together, you sat in bath, I told you, I told you.

CONNIE. . . . Just words.

CHARLEY. Aye . . . you, here, now, you'd be bloody torture, you are torture.

CONNIE. No.

CHARLEY. I can't miss what I've never had. An' I don't wanna start missing it, I can't be doing with knowing or understanding that stuff. I'm happy as I am. An' neither can you.

CONNIE. No.

CHARLEY. You wanna be in here knowing . . . if you do love me –

CONNIE. I do.

CHARLEY. If you do, then you won't come back. Please.

CONNIE. . . . I do love you.

CONNIE starts to put her coat on, preparing to leave.

An' you still think your flowers are for Tracey? Charley, they're for us.

CONNIE leaves.

Scene Ten

Time passes to much later in the evening. The orange streetlights finding a way in. CAROLINE *is on her own sat out on veranda. She wanders back into the kitchen and goes to the player as if about to put the music back on when she thinks better of it. She is thinking, troubled thinking, can't make her mind up, her hand wavers over the player a moment before deciding definitely not to. She doesn't know what to do. Her legs almost seem to be paining her through all the standing and she just lets it all go, she sits on floor propped against cupboard trying to let everything go from her head . . .*

RICHARD *enters, quietly, expecting to find her in kitchen but not sat on floor. He sees CD and makes no reaction. He approaches her, she looks up . . . there is a slight distance between them.*

RICHARD. How long you been there?

CAROLINE. Dunno. You been gone long time. Even pool hall don't stay open this late.

RICHARD. Haven't you done any revision?

CAROLINE. No.

RICHARD. You should.

CAROLINE. You not pissed?

RICHARD. No I'm not.

CAROLINE. But you were down pool hall.

RICHARD. Could do wi' you in here tomorrow.

CAROLINE. Gonna be hot?

RICHARD. Gonna be manic.

CAROLINE. Wish it'd right piss it down.

RICHARD. Aye . . . I think I got something to tell you.

CAROLINE. What?

RICHARD. . . . Gimme a moment.

CAROLINE. Alright . . . down pool hall, you win?

RICHARD. Is that giving me a moment?

CAROLINE. Sorry. You always win.

RICHARD. . . . No, I didn't win.

CAROLINE. You not win?

RICHARD. I need me moment here Caroline.

CAROLINE. What for?

RICHARD. Cos.

CAROLINE. Have yer moment.

RICHARD. . . . There. Had me moment. I didn't lose neither.

CAROLINE. Richard I don't get you.

RICHARD. I didn't go to pool hall.

CAROLINE. Where'd you go?

RICHARD. Feeling all sad an' desperate, went to club where we met.

CAROLINE. What you doing in that shit-hole? . . . It still magnet for underage kids is it?

RICHARD *nods, then laughs, after a moment* CAROLINE *laughs too, both laugh together – they share the moment and then the laughter dies as quickly as it came.*

Sorry.

RICHARD. It's true.

CAROLINE. Yeah. What'd you go there for?

RICHARD. I thought maybe I'll just do it all again. Not too old to have another one.

CAROLINE. You what?

RICHARD. Found meself thinking I'll replace you. Go back there, find meself 'nother sixteen year old, think I'm so

SCENE TEN 71

grown up wi' job and car an' I'll be her world, like you . . . and can you believe it this gorgeous girl wi' dress up her knickers, this kid, comes up to me an' we're talking like when me an' you . . . an' she says she eighteen.

CAROLINE. Oh . . .

RICHARD. You said you eighteen, then afterwards you said you seventeen, then later when I so in love wi' yer I can't help meself you say you fifteen . . . an' this kid looks in me eyes like you did an' says she eighteen. I got outta there so fucking quick.

CAROLINE. You weren't gonna, were you?

RICHARD. I were gonna, maybe.

CAROLINE. You been drinking?

RICHARD. I hadn't been. Just one. I only known you – my Caroline – just wanted to see how I remember you, try and help memory of what you like when you sixteen. Best time of my life that. You were sod everyone for me, yer Mam, yer mates. First time I met you, I thought gawd, this girl is everything.

CAROLINE. Aye.

RICHARD. But I were also thinking even then, god, what if she grows up? Or is this her grown up now, I didn't know. I thought I'll take chance. Me mates thinking phwoarh jammy bastard get her, and then they find she only fifteen, sad wanker. That why I lost me mates? Cos I could only pull a kid?

CAROLINE. I weren't a kid.

RICHARD. Yes you were.

CAROLINE. Was I?

RICHARD *nods*.

RICHARD. And I knew it. Fifteen, what are you at fifteen? I made you.

CAROLINE. No you didn't. Did you?

RICHARD. I dunno. I could paint you a picture of how it'll be at yer uni, how I'll slot in nice with your new friends, your new life, my old same life . . . nah.

CAROLINE. Nah?

RICHARD. Nah. All I can worry about now is the past.

CAROLINE. Richard, what you like?

RICHARD. I want you to think of me and smile like, I mean sure you'll frown bit an' all won't you, it's me isn't it, but I want you to smile most, when you think of me. Yeah?

CAROLINE. What you talking 'bout?

RICHARD. I do love you, so I'm gonna go.

CAROLINE. Go?

RICHARD. I not going wi' you, my transfer. I'm not taking it.

CAROLINE. What 'bout yer transfer, 'bout yer –

RICHARD. You should be pleased, I should be pleased, but I can see you in bar wi' yer new friends, and you'll actually hopefully have some friends, they'll look at me an' think what she doing wi' him. Young lads wi' their cocks doing overtime be thinking she'll forget him. They be right.

CAROLINE. No!

RICHARD. Yes! Fucking yes!

CAROLINE. If it were yer own place you'd feel different.

RICHARD. But it isn't gonna be. Just me like I am here.

CAROLINE. Just students.

RICHARD. Aye an' any of little gobshites gimme crap I'd, I'd . . . it's all about you, all of me is all about you . . . I tired of it . . . you making me hate me'self.

CAROLINE. Richard . . .

RICHARD. You are . . .

CAROLINE. You staying here? . . . What?

RICHARD. Nothing.

CAROLINE. Well are you?

RICHARD. No! You think I'm staying in this shit hole wi' him?

CAROLINE. Where you going?

RICHARD. You not only one that can go.

CAROLINE. I'm one going! Where are you going?

RICHARD. Nought do wi' you.

CAROLINE. Richard . . .

RICHARD. I not telling you.

CAROLINE. Well what 'bout, what 'bout yer job?

RICHARD. I do this shit for you, you've kept me in this shithole . . . Caroline, I just want you to be happy, and you're not, are you?

CAROLINE. Dunno. You're all I known.

RICHARD. You know I miss me old happy Caroline so much.

CAROLINE. I know you do.

RICHARD. You're not her though.

CAROLINE. No. What will you do?

RICHARD. Don't care. Might go to Australia. Always wanted to. With money I saved for the move to uni I could . . . maybe. I dunno.

CAROLINE. Richard?

RICHARD. I'll think of something.

CAROLINE. When?

RICHARD. Pretty much now.

CAROLINE. . . . Now?

RICHARD. Well why not? Yeah?

CAROLINE. . . . I dunno.

RICHARD. Yeah. 'Fore I change me mind. Okay? Okay?

CAROLINE. . . . O . . . Okay.

RICHARD. Yeah, that problem isn't it? It is okay.

They nestle their heads in each other. They embrace and
CAROLINE *kisses him on the cheek.* RICHARD *breaks away and walks out into the kitchen.* CAROLINE *struggles but holds back the tears, sits on crate, arms wrapped round herself.*

Scene Eleven

Next day.

It is mid-evening. The pub outside is in full flow. CHARLEY *is sat out on veranda. No music plays, no fag smoked, nothing.* CHARLEY *is just staring ahead. Waiting.*

CAROLINE *enters from bar. She sees his CDs and coat are still there and she seems relieved. She looks in the CD player and gives a little smile. Sees* CHARLEY *through window. She hovers in the veranda doorway,* CHARLEY *realises she is there but doesn't move (at some point they move into the kitchen).*

CHARLEY. Hello Caroline.

CAROLINE. You alright? . . . I'm sorry about Connie.

CHARLEY. Aye.

CAROLINE. I dunno why, but, but if it gonna make you miserable, being happy, then you done right thing . . . maybe.

CHARLEY. I have.

CAROLINE. Aye. What fuck is being happy anyway?

CHARLEY. Fucked if I know. Are you alright?

SCENE ELEVEN

CAROLINE. Mmm. I think you are you know, happy, for moments, for a while, from time to time. Real happy. But that about it.

CHARLEY. Been manic.

CAROLINE. Aye, manicest I ever known it. Mind you, it would be wouldn't it without Richard. Turns out he kept it from being crazy fucking insane manic.

CHARLEY. I can't believe he's left you.

CAROLINE. Why?

CHARLEY. I didn't think he would. Would you have left him?

CAROLINE. I were about to. I think. Maybe.

CHARLEY. You know the bastard didn't say goodbye to me?

CAROLINE. I'm sorry he didn't.

CHARLEY. Loads of 'em have never said goodbye. Don't know why I'm surprised.

CAROLINE. He should have said goodbye to you.

CHARLEY. Had it in me head how we'd all say goodbye. You'd both be loading car up, shaking hands, hugs like. A proper goodbye.

CAROLINE. Thought you were used to people leaving?

CHARLEY. Well, you been here a while haven't you?

CAROLINE. Good it bein' manic, keep me busy.

CHARLEY. You missed your classes.

CAROLINE. Weird being here without him.

CHARLEY. Your classes.

CAROLINE. But I wanted to keep busy.

CHARLEY. That's not the bloody point though, is it? . . . You can't keep missing 'em.

CAROLINE. I won't, from tomorrow it be no problem.

CHARLEY. They're important.

CAROLINE. I know they bloody well are.

CHARLEY. They are.

CAROLINE. From tomorrow I'll be at every single bloody one, an' all the extra ones they put on. I will.

CHARLEY. Aye. Make sure you . . . you're going too aren't you?

CAROLINE. I am. Moving back in with me Mam for a few month, do me exams.

CHARLEY. You do right. Soon?

CAROLINE. Well now. Me Mam's coming for me. I'm all packed up. Haven't got much to pack.

CHARLEY. Right. So when you get into yer university where you think you be living now?

CAROLINE. I be in hall I reckon.

CHARLEY. Wi' friends?

CAROLINE. Hope I make some.

CHARLEY. You will. An' what you think you do wi' all these exams you gonna get then?

CAROLINE. That's years away.

CHARLEY. I'd like some idea. Teacher?

CAROLINE. I dunno. Richard liked to have a game plan to work to so I had to give him one. He liked plans . . . Richard liked . . .

CHARLEY. What?

CAROLINE. Richard, past tense – wow . . . just trying the sound of it out. Sorry. I haven't got any ideas what I'm gonna do. I'll go study an' be a waitress. Pretty much this then.

CHARLEY. Well whatever you end up doing, just do something won't you?

CAROLINE. Aye.

SCENE ELEVEN

CHARLEY. Be like old times in here, 'fore you and Richard, fucking chancers they be putting in 'ere. Some cocky little shit with a Napolean complex will be running it. Just what I chuffing need.

CAROLINE. You think they'll say manic? Keep our lingo?

CHARLEY. Nah. They'll change the words. They never stay the same.

CAROLINE. Oh.

CHARLEY. I hope they do change the words. Can't be doing with it. Service'll go right down the pan you watch an' all. Have to shut kitchen while they find us these buggers.

CAROLINE. Aye . . . you been listening to the daft Queen again?

CHARLEY. No I haven't.

CAROLINE. It's in the player. Why haven't you put it on?

CHARLEY. I listened to it enough.

He takes it out of the player, puts it in case and hands it to her.

Here . . . you have it.

CAROLINE. You sure?

CHARLEY. Well I know how much you like it.

CAROLINE. Ta.

CHARLEY. You alright.

CAROLINE. Well you listen to it too much you know, cos it isn't real, it nice and pretty and beautiful like, but it isn't real. Just in yer head.

CHARLEY. No it isn't real.

CAROLINE. Specially that Queen, cos she's daft you know.

CHARLEY. Aye.

CAROLINE. But I'm sorry I won't get to listen to no more of yer music, but it's right good.

CHARLEY. Mmm.

CAROLINE. Maybe I'll get to hear more on me own?

CHARLEY. Aye, maybe.

CAROLINE. . . . An' it isn't shit.

CHARLEY. It isn't shit.

CAROLINE. . . . I'm sorry about Connie . . . Me Mam be waiting now, come here. Let's do goodbye proper like eh?

She hugs him and after a moment of standing in her embrace CHARLEY *reciprocates and puts his arms around her and hugs her tight a brief moment, lets her go.*

CAROLINE. Goodbye Charley.

CHARLEY. Goodbye Caroline.

CAROLINE *leaves.*

CHARLEY *sits in his chair, looks at empty CD player a moment.*

End.

A Nick Hern Book

Got To Be Happy first published in Great Britain in 2003
as a paperback original by Nick Hern Books Limited,
14 Larden Road, London W3 7ST

Got To Be Happy copyright © 2003 Simon Burt

Simon Burt has asserted his right to be identified as
the author of this work

Typeset by Country Setting, Kingsdown, Kent CT14 8ES
Printed and bound in Great Britain by Bookmarque,
Croydon, Surrey

A CIP catalogue record for this book is available from
the British Library

ISBN 1 85459 746 9

CAUTION   All rights whatsoever in this play are strictly reserved.
Requests to reproduce the text in whole or in part should be
addressed to the publisher.

Amateur Performing Rights   Applications for performance in
excerpt or in full by non-professionals in English throughout the
world (with the exception of the United States of America and
Canada) should be addressed to: Nick Hern Books, 14 Larden Road,
London W3 7ST, *fax* +44 (0)20-8735 0250,
e-mail info@nickhernbooks.demon.co.uk – except as follows:

Australia Dominie Drama, 8 Cross Street, Brookvale 2100,
fax (2) 9905 5209, *e-mail* dominie@dominie.com.au

New Zealand: Play Bureau, PO Box 420, New Plymouth,
fax (6)753 2150, *e-mail* play.bureau.nz@xtra.co.nz

United States of America and Canada: Peters Fraser and Dunlop
(as below)

Professional Performing Rights   Applications for performance
by professionals in any medium and in any language throughout
the world (and by amateurs in the United Sates of America
and Canada) should be addressed to Peters Fraser and Dunlop,
Drury House, 34-43 Great Russell Street, London, WC2B 5HA,
fax +44 (0) 20-7836 9539

No performance of any kind may be given unless a licence has
been obtained. Applications should be made before rehearsals
begin. Publication of this play does not necessarily indicate its
availability for amateur performance.